HEALTH INSURANCE RESOURCE MANUAL

A Guide for People with Chronic Disease and Disability

HEALTH INSURANCE RESOURCE MANUAL

A Guide for People with
Chronic Disease and Disability

Dorothy E. Northrop, MSW, ACSW
Director of Clinical Programs
National Multiple Sclerosis Society

and

Stephen E. Cooper
National Coordinator, Health Insurance Information
National Multiple Sclerosis Society

New York

Demos Medical Publishing, Inc., 386 Park Avenue South, New York, New York 10016

© 2003 by Demos Medical Publishing, Inc. All rights reserved. This book is protected by copyright. No part of it may be reproduced, stored in a retrieval system, or transmitted in any form or by any means, electronic, mechanical, photocopying, recording, or otherwise, without the prior written permission of the publisher.

Northrop, Dorothy E., 1942–
　Health insurance resources : options for people with a chronic disease or disability / Dorothy E. Northrop, Stephen Cooper.
　　　p. ; cm.
　　ISBN 1-888799-69-2
　　1. Insurance, Health. 2. Chronically ill. 3. Medically uninsured persons. 4. People with disabilities. 5. Social medicine.　I. Cooper, Stephen, 1946– .　II. Title. [DNLM: 1. Insurance, Health—United States—Handbooks.　2. Insurance, Health—United States—Resource Guides.　3. Chronic Disease—United States—Handbooks. 4. Chronic Disease—United States—Resource Guides. 5. Disabled Persons—United States—Handbooks. 6. Disabled Persons—United States—Resource Guides. 7. Medically Uninsured—United States—Handbooks. 8. Medically Uninsured—United States—Resource Guides.　W 49 N877h 2003]
　　RA413.7.U53N675 2003
　　368.4'2'00973—dc21
　　　　　　　　　　　　　　　　　　　　　　　　　　　　　　　　　　　　　2002014051

Printed in the United States of America

■ Dedication

This book is dedicated to Pamela Cavallo, MSW, CSW, now deceased, who, as Director of Clinical Programs of the National Multiple Sclerosis Society, recognized that people with disabilities and pre-existing conditions must have understandable and usable health insurance information. It was her vision that this manual would maximize health insurance coverage, promote patient rights, and provide strategies and resources for people with chronic conditions as they negotiate our very complex health insurance system.

Acknowledgments

We extend appreciation to those who gave of their experience and expertise to review this manual.

Sharon Finn, CCM, RN, MS
Former Chapter Programs Director
Greater Connecticut Chapter, NMSS

Charles D. Goldman, Esq.
Former General Counsel
U.S. Access Board

Peter Kennedy, B.S.
Chapter Programs Director
Greater Delaware Valley Chapter, NMSS

Deanna J. Okrent, M.P.A.
Former Assoc. Director, 1995 White House Conference on Aging
Consultant, National Ombudsman Resource Center

Jennifer Ricklefs, MS
Manager, Knowledge & Family Programs
National Multiple Sclerosis Society

Appreciation is also expressed to Deborah Kooperman, member of the Greater Delaware Chapter of the National Multiple Sclerosis Society, for her contribution to the material on Social Security Disability Insurance.

Contents

Preface   xi

1 Health Insurance Managed Care and Indemnity Plans   1

Historical Overview   1
What Is a Fee-for-Service or Indemnity Plan?   2
What Is Managed Care?   3
Managed Care Plans   3
Definitions, Terms, and Features of Managed Care   6
Managed Care versus Traditional Indemnity Health Insurance   9
Grievances and Appeals   10
Managed Care—Advantages and Disadvantages   16
Health Insurance Policy Checklist   18
Health Insurance Tips   19
Potential Sources of Insurance Coverage to Explore   20
Defined Contribution Plans   21

2 Medicare   23

Parts A, B, and C Coverage   23
Services Not Covered Under Medicare   26
Medicare PPO Demonstration Project   27
Financial Assistance for Medicare Program Costs   28
Medigap   28

3 Medicaid   31

Eligibility   31
Service Coverage   32
Medicaid and Managed Care   33

4 Social Security Disability Insurance   37

Application   38
Appeals   39
Attorney Fees   42
Trial Work Period   43
Medicare Eligibility   43

5 Supplemental Security Income   45

Financial Eligibility   45
Application   47
Disability Determination   47
Appeal   48
Medicaid Coverage   49
Attorney Fees   51

6 SSDI/SSI: The Application Process   53

Step 1: Description of Disability   53
Step 2: Work History   57
Step 3: Physician Contacts   57
Step 4: Filing Application   57

7 Employee Retirement Income Security Act   59

ERISA Pre-emption   59

8 Health Insurance Portability and Accountability Act   63

Guaranteed Protections   63
Pre-existing Condition   64
Non-Discrimination Based on Health Status   65
Certificate of Coverage   65
Modification of Employee Retirement Income
   Security Act (ERISA) Preemption   66
Modifications to COBRA   67
Long-term Care Insurance   67
Medical Savings Account   67
Health Care Fraud   68
Privacy   69
Summary   69

- **9** Consolidated Omnibus Budget
   Reconciliation Act of 1985   71

   Qualifying Events   72
   Covered Benefits   73
   Notice and Election Procedures   75
   Cost of Coverage   76
   Certificate of Coverage   77

- **10** State "Mini-COBRA" Laws   79

   "Mini-COBRA" Laws in Effect in 40 States   80

- **11** Ticket to Work and Work Incentives
   Improvement Act of 1999   91

   Overview of Legislation   91
   The TWWIIA Act   91
   Incentives to States   92

- **12** Comprehensive State Health Insurance
   for High-Risk Individuals   93

   Appendix 1: Insurance Directory   143

   Appendix 2: Useful Web Sites   165

   Appendix 3: Definition of Key Acronyms   169

   Appendix 4: State Pharmaceutical Assistance Programs   171

   Appendix 5: State Children's Health Insurance Program   187

   Index   189

Preface

Health insurance is one of society's most pressing issues. The United States is the only industrialized nation in the world that does not provide health insurance for everyone. The uninsured as well as those with inadequate health insurance coverage are increasing at alarming rates. In 1992, 38 million people in this country were without health insurance. Today it is estimated that over 43 million Americans lack health insurance coverage. Most of the uninsured are under 65 years of age, as Medicare covers virtually all elderly Americans (Kaiser Commission on Medicaid and the Uninsured).

In addition to the uninsured, millions of people have health insurance that is inadequate to meet all of their health care needs, particularly those with chronic disabilities. In an informal survey of people with multiple sclerosis (MS), the most frequently cited unmet needs included:

- Medications
- Home care
- Rehabilitation services (physical therapy, occupational therapy)
- Durable medical equipment
- Mental health counseling

It is expected that these same problems occur with a range of other chronic disorders.

There are many causes for this lack of adequate insurance coverage. These include:

- Refusal by some health insurance companies to sell insurance to people with pre-existing illnesses and disabilities.
- Seriously restricted coverage for some people with pre-existing illnesses and disabilities.
- Unemployment, self-employment, or employment by small companies that cannot afford to offer health insurance coverage.

- Changes in people's life circumstances—divorce, separation, death of a working spouse.
- Widespread lack of knowledge about insurance options and lack of understanding about how to make one's way through the health insurance system.
- Gaps and weaknesses in the system.

Drastic changes are needed in the United States health insurance system. These changes may take years to accomplish, however, as most change is incremental in nature. In the meantime, we need to make the current system work better. We need to disseminate information about insurance options and increase people's understanding of how to make their way through our complex insurance system.

This book contains information about a wide variety of options that will be of assistance to individuals who are uninsured, underinsured, or who have questions about insurance and don't know where to begin. The first section presents an overview of health insurance plans, Social Security, Medicare, Medicaid, and federal legislation that impacts health insurance coverage. The second section includes directories and resources to assist in researching health insurance options.

This book was developed to assist people with disabilities and chronic health conditions, and health care professionals, to understand the health care system and can maximize rights and entitlements within that system. It is important that this information be supplemented and updated with local and state legislation and regulations on an ongoing basis.

Dorothy E. Northrop, MSW, ACSW
Director of Clinical Programs
National Multiple Sclerosis Society

Stephen Cooper
Coordinator, Health Insurance Information
National Multiple Sclerosis Society

Some of the features of a PPO include:

- Offering more services than provided by an HMO, thus making the care more costly;
- Requiring a co-payment for each visit that is generally higher than the HMO co-payment;
- Imposing an annual deductible and a higher total out-of-pocket cost than an HMO; and
- Requiring prior approval frequently for hospitalization and certain outpatient procedures.

Health Maintenance Organizations

An HMO is the oldest form of managed care. It is a prepaid health insurance plan that provides specified services for a fixed premium. In exchange, the insured will be entitled to comprehensive care, including doctor visits, hospital stays, emergency care, surgery, laboratory tests, X-rays, and therapy. The majority of the HMOs require the insured to pay, at most, a small co-payment when seeing an in-network doctor, charge no deductible, and require only a few out-of-pocket expenses as long as the doctors, hospital, or other providers that are used are part of the HMO. Some of the other features of HMOs include:

- Having the insured either choose or be assigned a primary care physician (PCP) within the network who monitors the individual's health and provides most of the medical care.
- Empowering that physician with the responsibility of referring the insured to a specialist or other health care provider when necessary.
- Utilizing a gatekeeper model that does not cover the cost of a specialist or other health care provider unless approved by the PCP.
- Utilizing a non-gatekeeper model that does not require a referral from the primary care provider before utilizing a specialist.

Generally, with the exception of emergency treatment, if the insured obtains care without the PCP's referral in the gatekeeper model, or obtains care from a non-network provider, he or she may be responsible for paying the entire bill.

Types of HMOs

A. *Staff Model HMO*—In this plan, the physicians are salaried employees or partners of the HMO who may also receive bonuses, incentive payments, or a share of the

monthly, to purchase the policy, and pays charges up to the policy's deductible before insurance payments begin. After the deductible has been met, the insured will share approved medical costs with the insurance company; usually, 80 percent is borne by the company, the balance by the insured. Indemnity plans generally pay charges for prescription medications and tests, as well as for physicians and hospitals. It may not cover some charges for preventive care such as routine checkups.

There are two types of fee-for-service coverage: basic and major medical. Basic protection pays toward the cost of room and care while the insured is in the hospital. It also contributes to the cost of surgery, hospital services, and supplies such as prescribed medicine, as well as some doctor visits. Major medical insurance takes over when the benefits provided in basic coverage end. It covers the expense of lengthy, high-cost illnesses or injuries.

■ WHAT IS MANAGED CARE?

Managed care is a system of medical management in which patients, administrators, purchasers, and providers are linked together with the common goal of improving health care quality and reducing costs. It is a broad term encompassing many types of organizations, payment mechanisms, review processes, and collaborations.

In managed care health insurance plans, insurance companies contract with doctors, hospitals, laboratories, and other health-related facilities to meet health care needs. This linking of health care coverage with providers is the key to how the insured acquires and obtains care. The ease of access is determined by such components as the availability of medical services and their acceptability to the insured, the location of health care facilities, transportation, hours of operation, and the cost of care.

■ MANAGED CARE PLANS

Preferred Provider Organization

A Preferred Provider Organization, or PPO, is the form of managed care closest to an indemnity plan. The insurance company contracts with individual providers and groups to create a network of health care facilities and medical personnel. Members of a group can choose any physician they wish for medical care, but their co-payments are significantly reduced if they choose a provider in the PPO network. Co-payments are predetermined fixed amounts paid per visit, regardless of treatment received. Going outside the network means meeting an annual deductible and paying co-insurance on higher charges.

In 1910, Montgomery Ward and Co. provided a health insurance plan for its employees covering illness and injury. The plan is regarded as the nation's first group health insurance policy and paid weekly benefits equal to one-half the employee's weekly salary with a minimum benefit of $5 and a maximum of $28.85 per week, if the employee was unable to work due to illness or injury.

By the early 1930s, two approaches to health insurance were emerging. The first approach used the indemnity model[1] and the second was an elementary managed care model; the earliest Health Maintenance Organization (HMO) originated in 1929 at the request of the Los Angeles Department of Water and Power. However, the growth of health insurance was slow at first, with less than 10 percent of the population—12,000,000 by 1940—covered by some sort of health insurance. The majority of the plans were indemnity policies.

A major shift in medical coverage occurred just after World War II, when health insurance became an important component of employee benefit packages. As the competition for health insurance became more intense, insurance companies recognized that they could charge different rates for different sub-groups within the population. People who were employed were generally healthier than individuals who were unable to work and were, therefore, offered coverage at lower rates.

By the late 1960s, the cost of delivering health coverage had increased substantially, making it a priority to establish a cheaper yet more effective form of coverage. In 1969, the National Governor's Association proposed a national health insurance plan that would utilize HMOs to provide coverage and still contain the increase of health care inflation. The Nixon administration, searching for a model to minimize the role of government in managing health care, also saw HMOs as a way to reverse the practice of paying physicians and hospitals for illness rather than for health. The administration proposed legislation in 1971 providing planning and startup funds for HMOs. In 1973, Congress adopted the Health Maintenance Organization Act, designed to stimulate the formation of comprehensive prepaid health care programs.

In 1970, fewer than 2 million people, or less than 1 percent of the population, were enrolled in HMOs. Because the cost of health care escalated dramatically during the next 25 years and the expense of managed care was considerably less than indemnity insurance, by 1996, about 60 percent of Americans were enrolled in some sort of managed care health plan (the most common of which were HMOs).

■ WHAT IS A FEE-FOR-SERVICE OR INDEMNITY PLAN?

An indemnity plan provides specific cash reimbursements for covered services, and any medical provider can be used. The insured pays a premium, usually

---

[1] Indemnity Model—Traditional health insurance coverage in which physicians, patients, or health institutions send medical bills to the insurance company for payment—classic "fee-for-service."

1

HEALTH INSURANCE: MANAGED CARE AND INDEMNITY PLANS

■ HISTORICAL OVERVIEW

Not too long ago, most people with health coverage went to whatever physician they wanted whenever they wanted and their insurance company reimbursed them a certain amount of their medical bills. Health care consumers or employers had to pay part of the price plus a hefty deductible. When this type of fee-for-service or indemnity plan became too expensive, managed care seemed like a good solution because it promised to deliver affordable quality care if consumers, doctors, and hospitals agreed to certain cost-containing restrictions.

Although managed care was not viewed as a viable health insurance option until the mid-1990s, the concept is not new. In fact, its origins can be traced to the early 1900s. Other forms of health coverage existed some 100 years earlier.

The earliest form of health services in the United States dates to 1798, when Congress established the U.S. Marine Hospital Services for seamen. Compulsory deductions for hospital services were made from the salaries of the sailors.

Early insurance policies frequently protected against lost income due to accidents. The first accident policy, written by the Franklin Health Assurance Company in 1850, provided that for a 15 cent premium, the policy would pay the bearer $200 in the case of an injury caused by a railway accident. If the accident caused total disability, the bearer would receive $400.

profits. Typically, doctors in all common specialties needed to deliver comprehensive care staff the organization. Such HMOs may even own their hospital systems, though more typically they contract with hospitals and other in-patient entities in their communities to provide non-physician services. This model affords greatest control over the practice patterns of physicians and typically offers "one-stop shopping" to outpatients because a wide range of services is available at the clinics.

- Advantages: Plan allows for a tight management of services and one-stop shopping.
- Disadvantages: The model may be difficult and expensive to establish, the range of care may be limited, and the network is restricted.

B. *Group Model HMO*—In this plan, the HMO contracts with a multispecialty physician group to provide all physician services to the HMO's members. Unlike the staff model, however, the group rather than the HMO employs the physicians. The best known HMO of this kind is the Kaiser Foundation Health Plan. Permanente Medical Groups provide all physician services for Kaiser members under an exclusive contract, while the Kaiser Foundation Health Plan does the HMO functions of marketing, enrollment, and collection of premiums.

- Advantages: Plan allows for a tight management of services and maintains lower overhead costs than found in the staff-model plans.
- Disadvantages: The model may be difficult and expensive to establish, the range of care may be limited, and the network is restricted.

C. *Network-Model HMO*—This plan generally contracts with more than one physician group and may contract with single or multispecialty groups. Physicians in the model are often required to undergo utilization reviews and other forms of oversight.

- Advantages: Plan allows for a tight management of services and maintains lower overhead costs than found in the staff-model plans.
- Disadvantages: The model may be difficult and expensive to establish and the range of care is restricted.

D. *Individual Practice Association (IPA)*—An organization of individual medical practices formed for the purpose of negotiating with an HMO. Typically, the HMO pays the IPA a single capitated fee, and leaves provider reimbursement to the IPA.[2] In this plan, physicians continue to practice in their own locations using their own staff.

---

[2] A capitated fee is a specified amount paid to a health provider for a group of specified health services. Amounts are determined by assessing a payment "per covered life" or per member. The amount of payment is fixed regardless of the nature of services delivered.

- Advantages: Plan allows for a very broad participation by community physicians; easier and cheaper to establish.
- Disadvantages: Management of physician behavior is limited.

Point-of-Service Plan

Many HMOs offer an indemnity type option known as a Point-of-Service or POS Plan. This plan has an out-of-plan provision that offers specified coverage under special circumstances for use of nonparticipating providers. This can be especially important to enrollees with medical conditions who may desire specialists beyond those available through the HMO.

In an HMO POS Plan, the use of in-network services must be approved by a primary care physician (unlike a managed care PPO or Preferred Provider Organization where the patient selects any type of covered care from any in-network provider). When going out-of-network with the POS plan, referral by the PCP means that the HMO will pay all or most of the bill.

■ DEFINITIONS, TERMS, AND FEATURES OF MANAGED CARE

There are certain definitions, terms, and features associated with managed care that are used in shaping the parameters of a particular plan. They include:

- *Gatekeepers or primary care physician:* Access to services in managed care is often controlled by a gatekeeper, typically a PCP who is responsible for overseeing and coordinating all aspects of a member's care and treatment. Pre-authorization must generally be obtained from the PCP before a member is referred to a specialist for surgery or hospitalization. Members of an HMO and of some PPOs are required to choose a PCP or one will be assigned.
- *Pre-existing condition:* A condition (whether physical or mental), for which medical advice, diagnosis, care, or treatment was recommended or received within the six-month period prior to the enrollment date.

    Under HIPAA, group health plans and insurers can only apply pre-existing exclusions to a plan member or dependent who:

    - Does not enroll during the first period the individual is entitled to join;
    - Does not enroll during a special enrollment period when there is a change in family status or loss of group coverage under another plan;
    - Has never had health coverage;

- Has previously had health coverage but for less time than the pre-existing exclusion period under the plan; or
- Has been without coverage for more than 63 days.

(Note that the exclusion period cannot extend for more than 12 months [or 18 months for late enrollees] after the enrollment date for conditions treated within six months prior to the enrollment.)

- *State Modifications to the Health Insurance Portability and Accountability Act (HIPAA):* States are required to pass insurance laws that conform to the federal provisions of HIPAA. There is flexibility allowed, however, in the laws states adopt, particularly if the legislation is more generous to the individual. Some of these modifications might include:
  - A lookback period of less than six months in determining the existence of pre-existing conditions;
  - A shorter period to exclude pre-existing conditions from coverage (less than 12 months for regular enrollees and 18 months for late enrollees);
  - Longer periods for lapses in coverage;
  - Broader categories in which a pre-existing condition limitation cannot be imposed; and
  - Additional special enrollment periods.
- *Co-insurance and Co-pay:* Co-insurance requires the insured to share the cost of medical care. Under an 80/20 co-insurance provision, for instance, the health policy pays 80 percent of eligible medical charges above any deductible. The insured is required to pay the remaining 20 percent.

In the event of a large or catastrophic medical expense, the policy may include a co-insurance cap or stop-loss limit. This provision places a limit on the insured's out-of-pocket costs in a given year arising from the operation of the co-insurance clause. The annual cap generally ranges from $2,000 to $3,000, and once reached, all eligible expenses will be paid in accordance with the terms of the policy up to the plan's overall limit of coverage.

Under a *co-payment* or *co-pay provision*, the insured is usually required to pay a set or fixed dollar amount (e.g., $10) each time a particular medical service is used. Co-pay provisions are frequently found in HMO or PPO plans, with a nominal co-payment applied to each office visit and to each prescription drug purchased.

- *Deductible:* The deductible is the portion of eligible medical expenses that the participant must pay before the plan will make any benefit payments. Generally, the higher the deductible, the lower the premium of the health plan. Most non-HMO medical plans (e.g., Indemnity, PPO, POS plans) have deductibles. Once the insured has paid the deductible, the insurance plan starts to pay the scheduled amount for all future covered expenses.

- *Open and closed formulary*: A *formulary* is a list of drugs approved by a health plan and is intended to be based on the most cost-effective method of treatment. Some health plans require physicians to prescribe only those drugs listed in their formularies; others allow more flexibility.

  In an *open* formulary, which is most common in non-HMO settings, physicians and pharmacies are often provided with financial incentives to use specific drugs on the formulary list, but the insured does not incur any financial penalties for using non-formulary drugs. In *closed* programs, which are most prevalent in HMO plans, non-formulary drugs are not covered at all.

- *Maximum out-of-pocket*: A maximum out-of-pocket limit is the maximum dollar amount the insured will have to pay for covered medical expenses during a specified period, generally per plan year. For instance, if a plan has an out-of-pocket limit of $1,000, the insured will not pay more than that amount for covered medical expenses. The out-of-pocket limit can be reached by accumulating (1) co-insurance amounts only or (2) co-insurance and deductibles. In determining how the amount will be accumulated, neither method is superior to the other; however, it is clearer and less complex to describe the word "maximum" as the maximum number of dollars the insured will pay. The maximum is usually expressed as two numbers, such as $3,000/$6,000. This means that a single insured will face an annual maximum of $3,000, while an insured, who includes his or her spouse in the plan, or a single insured with covered dependents will face $6,000 of otherwise eligible expenses per year. The family maximum is generally two to three times the single amount.

- *Open enrollment*: A period of time when eligible subscribers may elect to enroll in, or transfer between, available programs providing health care coverage. Under an open enrollment requirement, a plan must accept all who apply during a specific period each year. To find out more about the open enrollment policy in a particular state, contact either the Department of Insurance or the State Health Insurance Assistance Office. The telephone numbers for both are listed in the Insurance Directory that is located in Table 2.

- *Prior authorization*: Approval that must be secured from an insurance company before receiving a medical treatment, test, or surgical procedure. This means the insurance company will determine the medical necessity of the medical intervention.

- *Premium*: Amount of money an individual and/or an employer pays, usually monthly, to procure health insurance coverage.

- *Lifetime maximum*: Maximum amount of benefits available to a member during his or her lifetime. All benefits furnished are subject to this maximum unless stated as unlimited.

■ MANAGED CARE VERSUS TRADITIONAL INDEMNITY HEALTH INSURANCE—SOME OF THE SIGNIFICANT DIFFERENCES

A. *Choosing a physician*—Under an indemnity policy, those covered are given the option of selecting any physician they want to see, whenever they decide it is necessary. In managed care, the policyholders are either limited in whom they may see (the situation of an HMO) or are given a strong financial incentive to select only those doctors affiliated with the plan (a PPO).

B. *Consulting a specialist*—Under managed care, the PCP usually determines whether a specialist is appropriate, weighing the cost of the specialist with the need for such care. If a PCP does not refer the insured to a specialist, some plans (i.e., a PPO) allow for self-referral. Generally, in the non-gatekeeper plan, one can self-refer without penalty. In the gatekeeper plan, one cannot self-refer and receive payment. In a traditional plan, the insured can see any specialist whenever he or she feels it is necessary.

   Providers that are within a network usually negotiate a special rate with the managed care company. Therefore, it is important to remember that if a Managed Care Organization (MCO) pays 100 percent of reasonable and customary fees if one remains in-network, and 80 percent out-of-network, the difference may be more than 20 percent as the out-of-network provider can charge whatever fee he or she chooses.

C. *Periodic check-ups*—Under indemnity coverage, it has been reported that only one-third of such plans pay a percentage of the cost of a check-up. In managed care, since the emphasis is to prevent future complications, the cost of a check-up by a PCP is paid for by the plan.

D. *Method of payment*—In an indemnity plan, the insured will have to first satisfy the annual deductible before qualifying for any reimbursement. Once met, the insured will probably be expected to pay the physician's bill up front and later submit a claim to the insurer to be reimbursed for a certain percentage of the amount incurred (usually 80 percent). Under managed care, the insured will be charged a co-payment, usually between $5 and $20, which is generally expected to be paid at the provider's office. It is the provider's responsibility to file the necessary paper work.

E. *The quality and qualifications of physician*—Under managed care, the plan assumes some of the responsibility in determining whether a physician is qualified when invited to join the network. It has been reported that over 80 percent of the doctors participating in managed care are board certified. In an indemnity plan, it is generally the insured who must check the physician's qualifications and credentials and, having chosen one, make certain that appropriate care is being administered.

F. *Monitoring a member's satisfaction*—Under managed care, plans frequently solicit the opinions of participants as to the quality of care offered. In a traditional plan, monitoring the satisfaction level is often left to the insured. If the insured has a complaint, it is left to him or her to contact the provider directly.

■ GRIEVANCE AND APPEALS

Every managed care plan must provide a procedure for the insured to challenge the decision of the insurer when it denies coverage for services that the insured and/or his doctor believe are medically necessary. The extent of this procedure depends on whether the plan is a self-insured employer plan or purchased from an insurance provider. States regulate the business of insurance, which includes HMOs, PPOs, or other types of MCOs that sell a health insurance policy to an individual, employer, or other purchaser. The federal government, pursuant to the federal statute ERISA (Employee Retirement Income and Security Act—see page 59), regulates private sector employer health plans, including managed care plans that are administered by a private employer.

Self-Funded Plans—The Impact of ERISA

In a self-funded or self-insured group health plan, employers set aside funds to pay the health claims of their employees. By collecting the premiums, determining the benefits, and paying the claims, the employer assumes the total risk and financial responsibility of their employees' health insurance coverage. No insurance company is involved unless it is contracted to administer the paperwork. Approximately 48 million employees, or 39 percent of the workforce who are insured, are covered by self-funded plans.

Self-funded plans evolved following passage in 1974 of the Employee Retirement Income Security Act (ERISA). Although this federal legislation focused on protecting the solvency and security of employee pension plans, an unintended benefit was the pre-emption of self-funded employer plans from state regulation and legislation.

Under ERISA, a self-funded employer plan must provide adequate notice in writing to any participant or beneficiary whose claim for benefits under the plan has been denied. The notice must explain the reasons for the denial and provide a reasonable opportunity for a full and fair review of the decision by the party that denied the claim.

Under ERISA, beneficiaries whose benefits have been wrongfully withheld are entitled only to equitable relief and monetary damages. In practical terms, the claimant's recovery is limited to the value of the denied service or the service itself. In other words, punitive damages may not be part of an award.

The federal regulations governing ERISA provide that plans subject to the statute have 90 days from the date a claim is received to respond, if denied. The notice must explain the specific reasons for the denial and be written in a manner calculated to be understood by the claimant. A claimant is then allowed 60 days after receipt of the denial to request a review. A decision on the review must ordinarily be made within 60 days after the request for a review, unless special circumstances (such as the need to hold a hearing if the plan provides for a hearing) require an extension of time.

ERISA exempts self-funded plans from state regulation. Although the states have been much more innovative in using their regulatory authority to protect consumers during the grievance process, such reforms do not apply to the ERISA plans. For instance, current ERISA grievance and appeal rules do not distinguish between the types of claims for benefits under review (e.g., emergency vs. non-emergency services) nor require external appeal procedures. ERISA simply requires that plans provide a "meaningful" and "timely" procedure for hearing and resolving complaints. In other words, there is no federal standard that prescribes how complaint and appeal systems are to be structured and administered.

Insurance Coverage Purchased from an Insurance Company or Other Entity—State Regulated

Contrary to what the average consumer might consider to be fact, it is the states and not the federal government that have assumed the initiative in protecting patient rights in managed care. A state's commissioner of insurance is a source of specific information about patient protections in a state.

Some states have passed highly innovative laws to protect patient rights. For example, Maryland has enacted legislation that offers patients and health care providers state assistance in filing complaints with insurance companies. Other states are proposing laws on the types of grievance and appeals process insurance companies must offer patients when benefits are denied.

The following briefly describes recent state legislation impacting on the grievance and appeal process:

- *Alaska*—Alaska adopted a patient's bill of rights that includes provision for a fair, prompt, and mutual dispute resolution process in the case of a dispute between the MCO and the insured. This includes the availability of an external appeal process, the cost of which must be paid by the insurer.
- *California*—California amended its grievance procedure for denied claims to include the following:
    - The plan must specify the location(s) and telephone number(s) where grievances may be submitted. It must also furnish enrollees with written

responses to grievances. If the grievance involves an adverse determination, the insurer's response must include all criteria and clinical reasons used in supporting the decision. The insurer must retain copies of all grievances and responses for at least five years.

- California has also approved an external review procedure for experimental or investigational therapies pertaining to diseases that cause serious disability. The review must pertain to the denial of coverage of a specific drug, device, procedure, or other therapy that would have been covered except for the insurer's determination that the treatment is experimental or investigational.

- *Delaware*—Delaware enacted legislation providing, as a final step in the grievance process, a review of the denial by the State Independent Review Organization. The purpose of this agency is to review appealed issues of medical necessity if requested by the insured or their representative, as an external process after all appeal alternatives have been exhausted.

- *Hawaii*—Hawaii's statute provides that, if the enrollee requests expedited process and the circumstances meet the statutory standard, both internal and external appeals must be reviewed within 72 hours from the time they are submitted. Approval must be granted if the usual 45-day process, standard for either type of appeal, might seriously jeopardize the "health, life, health status, or maximum function" of the insured.

  The statute also mandates that a final internal determination will be subject to external review by a state panel, if requested by the enrollee. The review panel must consider the following factors in its deliberations:

  - The terms of the managed care contract;
  - Whether the plan's medical director properly applied the medical necessity criteria;
  - All relevant medical records;
  - The clinical standards of the plan;
  - The information provided;
  - The attending physician's recommendation; and
  - The generally accepted medical guidelines.

- *Kentucky*—Kentucky's legislation provides that, in the event coverage is denied, the plan, in addition to stating the reason(s) for its decision, must include instructions on how to file a request for review. In the case of a review, the only person who may conduct it and determine whether the initial finding should be affirmed or denied is a physician who did not participate in the initial review. The legislation also includes a procedure permitting the introduction of new clinical information that might be relevant in reversing the earlier denial if an external review is held.

- *Maine*—The state's legislation establishes the right of enrollees to have their rejected claims assessed by an independent external review organization. Any decision rendered by this body will be binding on the carrier. The carrier must also pay the expenses of the review.
- *Maryland*—Maryland enacted legislation requiring that only physicians or a panel of medical experts may make grievance determinations. A panel is defined as a group of medical personnel, at least one of whom is a physician, who is either board certified or eligible in the same specialty as the service under review.
- *Massachusetts*—Legislation was enacted requiring the insurer, when a grievance is filed, to maintain a formal internal process that provides for adequate consideration and timely resolution of proceedings, including:
  - A system for maintaining records for each grievance filed by an insured, and the responses thereto, for a period of seven years;
  - The inclusion in the determination notice of a statement describing the insurer's formal grievance process and the procedure to be followed in obtaining external review;
  - The insurer's toll free number for assisting clients in resolving their grievances;
  - A written acknowledgment of receipt of the grievance within 15 days and a written resolution of each grievance within 30 days from receipt; and
  - A procedure to accept grievances by telephone, in person, by mail, or by electronic means.

  A grievance not properly acted on by the insurer within the above time periods will be considered decided in favor of the insured.
- *Michigan*—Michigan enacted legislation affecting the internal review process. In part, the statute provides the following:
  - No request for external appeal may be made until the parties have exhausted the internal grievance process. However, if the medical condition of the insured is such that a delay in time would jeopardize the life or health of the individual, the external review may begin concurrently with the internal review process.
  - The insured may begin the external review if the insurer has not been timely in issuing its determination.
  - A description of both the standard and external appeals process must be included in the notice of adverse determination. This description needs to state that the insured (or representative) has the right to furnish additional information for the organization's consideration.
- *South Dakota*—South Dakota enacted legislation providing that resolution of grievances may involve the use of a mediation service.

- *Virginia*—The state approved the following measures that amended the independent review procedure used to consider claim denials:
  - The legislation extended the number of working days that the Bureau of Insurance must notify the claimant that his/her request for appeal is approved from 3 to 5 days.
  - It extended the time frame in which the original review must be conducted from 5 to 10 working days.
  - It extended the number of days in which medical records may be provided to the Bureau of Insurance from 10 to 20 days.
  - It lowered the threshold for which a claimant can appeal a final adverse decision from $500 to $300.

Challenging an Adverse Decision

If an adverse determination is made on a claim, it is important to carefully review the health insurance contract and become a smart and savvy consumer. If the contract clearly states that a particular service is not covered, it is doubtful that any amount of appeals will reverse that. However, if the language is vague, refers only to "medical necessity," or reads that the service has coverage, claimants should follow every level of the appeals process, and do so as quickly as possible. The following steps should be taken to help resolve the problem:

- It is imperative to organize an argument demonstrating the reasons why the denial letter was in error.
- Assistance should be obtained from people who know how to structure a medical care appeal and are on the insured's side. These include the employee benefits manager, the claimant's physician, and personnel on the hospital staff. They can frequently help get the claims paid.
- The State Attorney General's office and Department of Insurance should be informed of the problem to give the appeal higher visibility.
- It should be determined if the state has an ombudsman to assist in the negotiating process.
- The claimant should promptly contact the MCO, advise it of the Department of Insurance notification, and request (a) the medical reasons why the claim was denied; (b) the names of those involved in the decision denying the claim; and (c) whether these individuals have clinical expertise in the areas of medicine relevant to the medical problem.
- The claimant must find out how the plan's appeal process works. This means reading the plan contract carefully and reviewing the appeal process with the

plan administrator, if necessary. For many complaints, the customer service representative may be able to resolve the problem over the phone.
- The claimant needs to get their doctor on their side. This includes having the doctor write the MCO explaining the reasons why the claim should be approved.
- A second opinion should be secured and/or obtain the names of other doctors recommending the type of treatment being requested.
- If not satisfied with the representative's response, a supervisor should be requested immediately.
- If the case is not an emergency, the plan's administrative review board should re-evaluate its initial determination. A letter of confirmation should be written, documenting which insurance representative agreed to send the matter to review, enclosing any other relevant material, and restating the action anticipated and the expectation that the review process will proceed expeditiously.

Sample Claim Appeal Letter

Date
Claim Representative's name   Claimant's name
Representative's address   Claimant's address
City State ZIP   City State ZIP
Dear Claim Representative:

This letter serves as a request for reconsideration of payment of a denied claim related to the treatment of my medical condition.

As your records will show, I was diagnosed with _____ in (*month & year*). [Insert information regarding medical history including previously attempted treatments and results.]

My neurologist (*or physician*), (*name of doctor*), wants me (to begin using the medication, _____,) (to begin a regimen of physical therapy), (to undergo a [*name of procedure*]), which he/she believes is necessary in the proper treatment of (*name of condition*). He/She has prepared a letter explaining the medical necessity of the (drug) (physical therapy) (procedure) in the proper treatment of the illness.

Based on the above information, I would appreciate your reconsideration of coverage for these submitted charges.

Sincerely,

If reconsideration is denied, a follow-up letter should be sent requesting the following information:

- The medical reasons why the claim was denied;
- The names and medical background of those individuals denying the claim;
- Whether these individuals have clinical expertise in your chronic condition or disability and the extent of their experience; and
- Further steps of appeal available.

State External Review

As of the end of 2001, forty-two states and the District of Columbia had enacted legislation creating external review as a means of resolving disputes between health plans and consumers. Almost all of these states require that the claimant first exhaust all of the health plan's internal grievance procedures before engaging in this external review process. However, once the internal review is completed, members have an option of having an independent review of their health plan's denial of coverage. Although this means a long process, and often a cumbersome one, almost half of the denials are overturned when plan members do pursue this course of action. The rate of overturn varies by state. Currently state external reviews apply only to members of insurance plans regulated by the state's Department of Insurance. Consumers covered by self-insured ERISA plans are not covered by state regulation and would need federal legislation for this option to be available to them.

■ MANAGED CARE—ADVANTAGES AND DISADVANTAGES

What are the advantages and disadvantages of managed care, and is it less costly and more effective than indemnity plans?

Advantages:

- Because MCOs think in terms of prevention rather than simple incidents, it is more likely to treat problems aggressively earlier if such treatment can avoid costly care later.
- MCOs are able to track patients over time and can provide information to PCPs earlier about patients at risk. This allows them to concentrate on the type of care needed to keep patients healthy with the intent of avoiding costly medical procedures in the future.
- Managed care offers a way of coordinating care through a central administration and common working system designed to reduce fragmentation. A common record system can improve the flow of information about an insured.

- An effective managed care operation simplifies the process of caring for a client and minimizes billing procedures and out-of-pocket expenses.
- Managed care has the opportunity of being more creative in developing ways to meet its service obligations. An example is the utilization of non-physicians to perform tasks normally assigned to physicians.
- In order to control costs, MCOs often negotiate fees with doctors, hospitals, and other health care providers. For example, most doctors give plans approximately a 20 percent discount off their usual fees. The incentive for the physicians and hospitals is a guaranteed patient pool. The plans then offer patients strong financial incentives—lower out-of-pocket costs—to encourage them to use the health care providers who are part of the network.
- MCOs often require health care professionals to coordinate the extent of health care provided to the insured with plan managers to reduce cost. This is intended to help the plan deliver appropriate care—neither too much nor too little—something fee-for-service or indemnity plans never claim to do.
- A number of managed care plans have designed systems to eliminate wasteful and duplicate medical tests that some experts say account for 30 percent of America's health care costs.
- If the MCO is an HMO, it most likely will use a PCP in its operation. One of the essential duties of the PCP is to monitor the use of physician-specialists who are not part of the HMO network. By restricting the use of specialists and creating alternative forms of care, money will be saved and costs contained.

Disadvantages:

- Many managed care programs require that patients see specialists only upon the referral of their PCP. PCPs may also monitor the specialists (including in-network), depending on the type of plan. This mandate may be simply a minor inconvenience to the insured, but it could become a major impediment if the PCP feels pressure to restrict access to specialists.
- The plan may not contract with the hospital the insured prefers.
- If the PCPs (or specialists) are judged on their use of laboratory testing, there will be pressure to avoid many tests in marginal situations. Many managed care programs use clinical protocols in establishing norms that are often very restrictive for ordering tests.
- When the benefit package includes drug coverage, consumers may find that certain medications are excluded because of high cost. At times, such individuals will be given a less expensive drug with more known side-effects before being offered drugs that have better results. Research also indicates that, if the insured

does not complain about the less expensive medication, he or she may not learn about the alternate medications.

- Just as fee-for-service has an incentive for too much service, managed care has an incentive to provide too little. In those instances where there is no clear-cut course of action on the best method of treatment, care often is based on dollars and cents. In other words, the less costly treatment may be used regardless of whether it is the best in a specific situation.

■ HEALTH INSURANCE POLICY CHECKLIST

When selecting health insurance, it must be remembered that the insurance is not only for treatment of the disease or disability that is of primary concern. Unless it is a specialized policy (i.e., catastrophic coverage), the insurance will pertain to all general health needs. It is, therefore, essential to exercise a great deal of care in the selection process. The following is a suggested list of questions to ask when buying health coverage:

- Are there waiting periods before certain illnesses are covered?
- How much is the deductible? Is the deductible for each treatment or illness, for each family member, or is it simply an annual deduction?
- Does the insured pay a certain percentage of costs (co-insurance) after the deductible has been satisfied?
- Must the insured pay a flat dollar amount (co-payment) for services such as doctor's office visits?
- What are the renewal conditions? Under what circumstances can the company increase the insured's premium?
- What is the maximum amount the policy will pay for each illness and for the entire time the policy is in force?
- What type of services does the policy cover? Will it pay for doctors' office visits or house calls?
- What is the pharmacy benefit and is referral required?
- What is not covered by the policy?
- What are the limits on:
  - The amount paid for daily hospital room and board?
  - The amount paid for medicine, tests, or other hospital expenses?
  - The amount paid for specific types of surgery?
  - The amount paid for doctors' visits?

- The maximum number of hospital days?
- The maximum number of doctors' visits during a hospital stay?

■ HEALTH INSURANCE TIPS

- *Be an educated consumer*—It is essential that you learn as much as you can about the types of policies that are available. It is no excuse to dismiss this point by saying that the presence of a pre-existing condition greatly limits the choices available. It is this limitation which makes it crucial to know that, although at a disadvantage, the quest for adequate and affordable coverage is not a pipe-dream and there are choices in coverage if you know the facts. You must become educated about the open enrollment policy of your state, whether the state offers high-risk insurance, the rules behind HIPAA and COBRA, the availability of coverage from an employer, group insurance offered by your alumni association or your business, professional and fraternal organizations, and, if applicable, whether a state has a mini-COBRA statute. Case managers can often be a valuable resource in accessing and maximizing insurance coverage.

- *Check agents and companies*—Make certain that the agent and company you are dealing with is licensed to sell insurance in the state where you reside.

- *Review applications*—You must make certain that any pre-existing conditions are listed on the applications if requested by the insurer and that all information is correct. False information or misrepresentation of health conditions in the application is against the law and may result in the denial of benefits or cancellation of the policy. If the insurance agent fills out the application and makes a mistake, tell the agent to complete another application. If you find a mistake after the application is forwarded to the company, notify the company in writing immediately. *Do not sign a blank application.*

- *Pay premiums annually*—You should check with your insurance agents about how much money can be saved by paying the premium one time during the year. You can avoid the service fee and possibly receive a discount for pre-payment.

- *Enroll in the employer's group health program*—The coverage available in a group plan is often more comprehensive and less costly than what an individual can buy on his or her own. If the employer does not have a group plan, encourage him or her to establish one.

- *Outline of coverage*—You should request an outline of coverage or a brief summary of what is covered under the policy before purchasing insurance. You can use the outline to compare coverage with other policies being considered at that time.

- *Review of policy after purchase*—You should read the entire Subscriber Agreement or Member Handbook carefully, and review your coverage at least once a year.

Handbooks can be secured from an employer's Department of Human Resources or benefits administrator. You need to read the fine print to make certain that the policies meet your own and your family's needs. Never assume that you are covered or not covered for something.

- *Pay by check only*—When purchasing an insurance policy, pay by check, money order, or bank draft made payable to the insurance company, not to the agent or anyone else. You should also get a receipt with the insurance company's name, telephone number, and address for your records.

- *Know with whom you are dealing*—An insurance company must meet certain qualifications to do business in a state. You should check with the state insurance department to make certain that any company being considered is licensed in the insured's state. This piece of advice is for your protection. Agents must also be licensed and may be required by the state to carry proof of licensure showing their name and the company they represent. If the agent cannot verify that he or she is licensed, do not buy from that person. A business card is not a license.

■ POTENTIAL SOURCES OF INSURANCE COVERAGE TO EXPLORE

- You may be eligible for employer's health insurance coverage.
- You may be able to obtain coverage under the spouse's insurance plan.
- You might be able to procure coverage through your states' high-risk insurance pool if you reside in one of the 29 states that offers such insurance. Under a high-risk plan, health insurance becomes available to the "hard or impossible" to insure. The drawbacks to this type of insurance are its higher cost, limited benefits, and waiting period that might be imposed before a policy is issued.
- Depending on the state where you reside, one might procure coverage during open enrollment periods. A number of states require all health insurance companies licensed to transact business to allow a resident to purchase a policy during a certain period of the year, regardless of pre-existing condition. Information on a state's open-enrollment policy may be obtained by contacting the state's insurance department or its health insurance assistance office. Telephone numbers for each state are listed in the section entitled "Insurance Directory."
- You might be able to procure group insurance through a professional, fraternal, membership, or political organization. An example of this type of organization is Working Today, a national not-for-profit open to individuals who are self-employed. Health insurance through this plan is currently available to members who reside in downstate New York.

- You might consider obtaining coverage through a health care coverage cooperative. A cooperative is a voluntary organization open to all persons able to use their services and willing to accept the responsibilities of membership without gender, social, racial, political, or religious discrimination. A cooperative is often associated with an agrarian interest, although the common thread among its members could be an association with any number of enterprises. An example of this type of organization is the Cooperative of Home Care Associates (CHCA), which is a for-profit, worker owned cooperative located in the South Bronx, New York.

- If you have coverage through an employer sponsored plan and have been temporarily or permanently laid off, voluntarily left the position, or had hours of work reduced (thus disqualifying you for coverage), the insurance might be extended through the federal Consolidated Omnibus Reconciliation Act of 1985 (COBRA). COBRA applies to companies with 20 or more employees. (See Chapter 9 for a detailed description of COBRA.)

  COBRA allows individuals to continue coverage at their own expense for 18 additional months at the group rate. Moreover, the federal Health Insurance Portability and Accountability Act (HIPAA) extends COBRA benefits for those individuals the Social Security Administration determines were disabled either before the COBRA event or within the first 60 days of COBRA continuation coverage. These individuals are entitled to 29 months of coverage.

- Forty states have adopted legislation providing COBRA-like protection to employees excluded from the federal law. A review of these policies can be found in the section entitled "Mini-COBRA" statutes.

■ DEFINED CONTRIBUTION PLANS

There is a current trend on the part of employers dealing with escalating health insurance costs to offer employees an insurance product as part of their benefit package called a *defined contribution plan*. These plans are based on the shifting of responsibility for payment and selection of health care services from the employer to the employee.

There is a wide variety of approaches to the defined contribution plan concept. In an extreme form, employers might terminate their group health plan and provide vouchers for employees to purchase their own coverage. In another model, employees would pay an annual premium, probably lower than under traditional plans, and would then receive an allowance of perhaps a few thousand dollars to spend on their medical expenses for the year, including drugs. Once they have spent that allowance, they would be required to cover all costs up to a determined amount, probably several thousand dollars, after which employers would again cover most of the expenses.

The advantage of these plans is that they are consumer-driven and give employees the incentive to carefully purchase their health care and receive the best value for the dollars they are spending. The disadvantage is that these plans favor those individuals who are healthier and have less medical expenses. Individuals with chronic medical conditions would almost always require health care beyond the initial allowance. There is also a concern that employees might forego certain preventive care and medical services based solely on financial reasons.

The defined contribution plan is a significant step away from the traditional insurance model that spreads risk across both the healthy and the sick. The traditional system is based on the concept that those members of a group who are ill will be covered by premiums paid by everyone else. The risk is shared. In the defined contribution plan, those with lower expenses are rewarded, while people with chronic medical conditions that are more costly must pay more out-of-pocket for their care.

■ 2

MEDICARE

In 1965 Congress established the Medicare program as Title XVIII of the Social Security Act. Enacted as one of President Lyndon Johnson's Great Society measures, its original intent was to be a federally funded system of health and hospital insurance for U.S. citizens age 65 or older. In 1973, the legislation was expanded to include individuals with disabilities who had been receiving Social Security benefits through the Social Security Disability Program for a period of 24 months.

■ PARTS A, B, AND C COVERAGE

Medicare consists of three parts—Part A is hospital insurance, Part B is supplementary medical insurance, and Part C covers managed care.

Medicare Part A

Medicare Part A is automatically provided to people who have been receiving Social Security Disability (SSD) benefits for at least 24 months. However, since individuals must wait five months from the time they become disabled before they are eligible to receive SSD payments, they in effect must wait 29 months before they have Medicare coverage; this is assuming that application for SSD was made at the onset of the disability.

Part A coverage includes hospital costs for semi-private rooms, meals, nursing services, operating room and recovery, in-patient prescription drugs, in-patient rehabilitation, intensive care, and laboratory tests, as well as limited coverage for medically necessary skilled nursing facility care and home health services.

To qualify for SSD benefits and Medicare, an individual must acquire the number of work credits required by law. The number of work credits needed by an individual for disability benefits depends on when the person becomes disabled. Generally, the applicant needs 20 credits earned in the last 10 years, ending with the year when the disability occurs. However, younger workers may qualify with fewer hours. (See Chapter 4, Social Security Disability for detailed explanation.)

Most people do not pay a monthly premium for Part A, because they have met the quarters of employment requirement (which includes self-employed work). If qualifications for premium-free Part A are not met, coverage may be purchased.

Part A does require Medicare beneficiaries to be subject to a deductible of $812 for hospital stays per benefit period. A benefit period begins the first day of an inpatient hospital stay and ends when the beneficiary has been out of the hospital or skilled nursing facility for 60 consecutive days.

For each benefit period, a Medicare beneficiary pays under Part A:

- A total of $812 for a hospital stay of one to 60 days.
- $203 per day for days 61 to 90 of a hospital stay.
- $406 per day for days 91 to 150 of a hospital stay.
- All costs for each day beyond 150 days.

Skilled nursing care—Medicare also provides some coverage for a skilled nursing facility (and home health care when medically necessary). The beneficiary is entitled to a semi-private room and nursing or rehabilitation therapies and for each benefit period pays:

- Nothing for the first 20 days;
- Up to $101.50 per day for days 21 to 100; and
- All costs beyond the 100th day in the benefit period.

Medicare Part B

Coverage under Medicare Part B is optional and is offered to all beneficiaries when they enroll in Part A. If the beneficiary decides to enroll, he or she is required to pay a premium of $54 per month in the year 2002; this may be increased in 2003.

Part B covers a variety of medical services and is often referred to as the Medical Insurance part of Medicare. Title XVIII of the Social Security Act restricts coverage and payment to only those services that are medically reasonable and necessary in accordance with accepted medical standards.

The medical expenses covered under Part B include:

- Physician services
- Inpatient and outpatient medical services and supplies
- Physical and speech therapy
- Diagnostic tests
- Ambulance services
- Radiology and pathology services (inpatient and outpatient)
- Up to 35 hours per week of medically necessary home health care
- Blood and urinalysis tests

Part B also pays for durable equipment in various ways. Some equipment must be rented while other equipment is required to be purchased. The Durable Medical Equipment Regional Carrier can provide more specific information. The telephone number for the local carrier may be accessed at *http://www.medicare.gov/contacts/home.asp.*

Medicare Part B has an annual deductible of $100. After this has been satisfied, Medicare generally pays 80 percent of the approved amount.

Medicare Part C—The Managed Care Option

Medicare Part C—also called Medicare + Choice—is an alternative to the traditional Medicare plan. It covers everything in Part A and Part B, but offers this coverage in a new manner that may take the form of a health maintenance organization (HMO), a preferred provider organization (PPO), a private fee-for-service (FFS) plan, a Medical Savings Account, or any other new type of health plan provided that it is authorized by Social Security.

Generally these plans operate on a "risk" basis, i.e., they receive a fixed payment from Medicare for each beneficiary enrolled in the plan. To remain profitable, they must provide the required health care services for less than they receive. Since 2001 these plans have faced huge challenges, as their reimbursement increased only 2 percent, compared with escalating health care costs in the double digits. Several companies offering Medicare + Choice plans have left the market, and those that continue to provide coverage have been reducing their benefits, particularly in the area of pharmaceutical coverage.

Except for emergency and urgently needed treatment, Medicare HMOs require the beneficiary to use only health care providers employed or contracted by the plan. Typically the beneficiary must select a PCP who acts as a gatekeeper for all health care services. Both the PCP and the managed care organizations are authorized to limit the plan's scope of services (i.e., the length of a hospital stay or the duration of post-hospital therapy services) or the beneficiary's access to specialists and hospitals.

This cost saving feature is also apparent in the case of a Medicare PPO. In a PPO, enrollees can choose any doctor, hospital, or specialist offered within the network. If they go outside the plan, however, they agree to share in the cost of care.

Under Medicare's managed care arrangement, plans are responsible for offering a basic package of medical services, comparable to those covered by parts A and B through a network of physicians, hospitals, and other medical providers. In addition, most plans choose to provide extra benefits. They often offer coverage of prescription drugs (generally limited to a fixed dollar amount), hearing aids, and other medical services not offered by traditional Medicare. The main advantage for the beneficiary is extended coverage and a single, predictable fixed monthly premium with few out of pocket expenses.

In some areas of the country, Medicare Part C also offers a beneficiary the option of being covered under an indemnity plan, referred to as a private FFS plan. The insurer, rather than the Medicare program, decides how much to reimburse for services provided. Some of the features of the plan include:

- Medicare pays a set amount of money every month to the private insurance company to cover traditional Medicare benefits.
- The beneficiary can go to any doctor or hospital that accepts the plan's payment.
- Providers are allowed to bill beyond what the plan pays (up to a limit) and the beneficiary may also be responsible for additional premiums.

(Please note that the various types of managed care plans are described in Chapter 1.)

Medicare + Choice is currently at a crossroads in terms of viability and its ability to continue to offer a managed care alternative to Medicare. Congress is aware of the challenges it is facing and is aware it will need to take steps to more aggressively support the program if it is to continue as a Medicare option. Approximately 14 percent of current Medicare enrollees are in the Medicare + Choice program.

■ SERVICES NOT COVERED UNDER MEDICARE

The following services are not covered by Medicare:

- Personal convenience items
- Private duty nurse
- Private room, unless it is medically necessary
- Routine physical examinations and tests related to exams
- Routine foot care including orthopedic shoes
- Dental services

- Cosmetic surgery
- Examinations for prescribing or fitting eyeglasses or hearing aids
- Eyeglasses or hearing aids
- Most immunizations
- Most prescription drugs
- Custodial care in nursing homes or at home
- Most chiropractic care
- Acupuncture
- Medical devices not approved by the U.S. Food and Drug Administration
- Services rendered outside the United States (Canada and Mexico may be an exception)

■ MEDICARE PPO DEMONSTRATION PROJECT

On January 1, 2003, Medicare will commence a demonstration project providing private fee-for-services plans to beneficiaries in 23 states.[1] Health plans that have been approved for participation have agreed to provide networks of preferred providers that will offer additional benefits to Medicare recipients. The program will be available to over 11 million beneficiaries and the insurance will be structured as a Preferred Provider Organization Plan (PPO).

Under a guideline released by the Department of Health and Human Services on August 27, 2002, although benefits offered in a particular state may differ from those provided in another state, some of the common features of the participating PPOs include:

- Networks of preferred providers (hospitals, physicians, and other providers) who provide all of the basic Medicare benefits, plus additional benefits such as annual physicals, other preventive services, disease management, and prescription drugs.
- Unrestricted access to doctors and hospitals without a referral.
- A balance of monthly premiums and some cost sharing amounts paid by the plan enrollees. For in-network services, the cost sharing amounts are lower than those for out-of-network services. In some cases, there are out-of-pocket maximums so when a maximum limit is reached, there is no more cost sharing.

---

[1] Alabama, Arizona, California, Florida, Illinois, Indiana, Kansas, Kentucky, Louisiana, Maryland, Missouri, North Carolina, Nevada, New Jersey, New York, Ohio, Oregon, Pennsylvania, Rhode Island, Tennessee, Virginia, Washington, and West Virginia.

- Fees paid to out-of-network providers will be no more than they would get in fee-for-service Medicare.
- Premiums will vary but will be priced between existing HMO premiums and premiums charged by Medigap or Medicare supplemental insurance products.

■ FINANCIAL ASSISTANCE FOR MEDICARE PROGRAM COSTS

States have programs that may pay some or all of Medicare's premiums and may also cover Medicare deductibles and co-insurance for certain people who have Medicare and a low income. To qualify, the beneficiary must have:

- Medicare Part A.
- No more than $4,000 as a single person, in liquid assets such as bank accounts, stocks, and bonds. A married couple may have up to $6,000 in such assets.
- A monthly income that is below certain limits (refer to chart below). Once a person or couple qualifies, they will be entitled to participate in the following programs:

Monthly Income Limits	Program Will Pay	Program Name
$759 Individual or $1,015 Couple (100 percent Federal Poverty Level)	Premiums, deductibles, and co-insurance	Qualified Medicare Beneficiary (QMB)
$906 Individual or $1,214 Couple	Medicare Part B premiums	Specified Low Income Beneficiary
$1,017 Individual or $1,364 Couple	Medicare Part B premiums	Qualifying Individual (QI-1)
$1,313 Individual or $1,762 Couple	A small part of the Medicare Part B premium	Qualifying Individual (QI-2)

For more information about these programs, you can either call your state's health insurance assistance number, which is the final item listed for each state in the Insurance Directory, or 1 (800) 633-4227 (toll free number for Medicare).

■ MEDIGAP

Medigap, also known as Medicare Supplemental Insurance, is insurance that supplements the basic coverage provided under Medicare and pays for health care costs that Medicare does not pay—such as deductibles and co-insurance. It is regulated by both federal and state law and, unlike other types of health insurance, it is designed specifically to supplement Medicare's benefits by filling in some of the gaps in Medicare coverage.

Congress standardized Medigap into 10 basic plans to ease the confusion over which policies offered which benefits. This rule allows beneficiaries to comparison shop, since insurance companies can only sell the same 10 basic policies. Premiums vary widely according to the plan selected, age, and state of residence.

The basic benefits offered under all plans include:

- Hospital co-insurance.
- Full coverage for 365 additional hospital days (to be used after exhaustion of Medicare hospital reserve days).
- Twenty percent co-payment for physician and other Part B services.
- Three pints of blood.

Each state must allow the sale of Plan A and all Medigap insurers must make Plan A available. Each of the other nine plans includes the basic plan plus a different combination of benefits. Although states are only required to allow the sale of Plan A, most offer several plans, and some offer all 10.

A number of benefits are available in the various plans, but each plan offers a variety of benefits and no one that offers all. These benefits include:

- Coverage of Medicare hospital deductible.
- Skilled nursing facility daily co-insurance.
- Coverage of Part B $100 deductible.
- Eighty percent of emergency medical costs outside the United States during the first two months of a trip.
- Payment to cover the difference when a doctor's fees are over the Medicare-approved charge.
- At-home care charges in addition to and in conjunction with Medicare approved home care.
- Some prescription drug coverage.
- Some preventive medical care coverage.

If someone is a new Medicare Part B subscriber and is 65 years of age, that person is given a six-month open enrollment period for Medigap policies. This means an insurance company cannot refuse to insure him/her because of a pre-existing condition. However, the company may make the beneficiary wait up to six months before filing claims for pre-existing conditions. A Medigap insurance company is also required by law to renew a Medigap policy if the premiums have been paid.

There is no federal law that requires insurance companies to sell Medigap plans to people under age 65. For regulations regarding Medigap policies available in your state, either voluntarily or because it is required by state law, contact your State Health Insurance Assistance Program.

3

MEDICAID

Title XIX of the Social Security Act is the statutory provision that created Medicaid, a Federal/State entitlement program that pays for medical assistance for certain individuals and families with low income and resources. One of its crucial roles is the financing of health and long-term care services for low-income individuals with disabilities. According to the Congressional Budget Office, Medicaid is the single largest source of health care financing—public or private—in the United States. Currently Medicaid covers approximately 36 million individuals.

Medicaid became law in 1965 as a cooperative venture jointly funded by the Federal and State governments (including the District of Columbia and the Territories) to assist states in furnishing medical assistance to eligible and needy persons. The services that Medicaid covers in most states, ranging from health services to personal attendant care to prescription drugs, are often critical to the ability of individuals to improve their capacity to function and become self-sufficient. Medicaid is also the primary public payer for long-term care, particularly in nursing homes. Medicaid's eligibility rules and benefits are generally structured to provide coverage for those with high levels of medical need and low income and assets.

■ ELIGIBILITY

Three basic groups are eligible for Medicaid:

- Low-income children and low-income parents with children;
- Adults aged 65 and older who are receiving cash assistance through the Supplemental Security Income Program (SSI); and
- People who are disabled, most of whom are eligible because they are receiving cash assistance through the SSI program. The remainder generally qualify

because they have incurred large medical expenses (i.e., hospital, prescription drugs, nursing home charges) thereby meeting their "spend down" obligation.[1]

Many people carry the misconception that Medicaid provides medical assistance to all poor persons. Even under the broadest provision of the Federal statute, Medicaid only becomes available to the very poor if they qualify for one of the groups specified by law.

In general, an individual must be an American citizen or a legal alien, meet state income or resource standards, and fit into a covered eligibility category. A person who is disabled, as defined by the Social Security Act, fits into a covered eligibility category.

The Social Security Act defines disability as "the inability to engage in any substantial gainful activity by reason of any medically determinable physical or mental impairment(s) which can be expected to result in death or which has lasted or can be expected to last for a continuous period of not less than 12 months."

■ SERVICE COVERAGE

Federal guidelines require coverage of a broad range of basic services. These include:

- Hospital care (inpatient and outpatient);
- Nursing home care;
- Physician services;
- Laboratory and X-ray services;
- Family planning services;
- Health center (FQHC) and rural health clinic (RHC) services; and
- Nurse practitioner services.

States also have the option of covering additional services and receiving federal matching funds for those services, which includes:

- Prescription drugs;
- Personal care and other community-based services for individuals with disabilities;
- Dental and vision care for adults;
- Diagnostic services;
- Clinic services;

---

[1] The Medicaid Act allows states to offer "medically needy" programs. A majority of the states have elected this option, thereby allowing individuals to spend down their incomes on necessary medical and remedial expenses as well as on premiums, deductibles, and co-payments charged or fixed by Medicare and other health insurance. Within these federal guidelines, states have considerable flexibility in establishing their own financial eligibility criteria.

- Transportation services; and
- Rehabilitation and physical therapy services.

Within broad federal guidelines and certain limitations, states are given the responsibility of deciding the amount to be spent and duration of services offered under a Medicaid program, subject to the following restrictions:

- A sufficient level of services must be provided to reasonably ensure the purpose of the benefits; and
- A limitation on a particular program may not have the effect of discriminating among beneficiaries based on medical diagnosis or condition.

Under Sec. 1915 of the Social Security Act, States may also request "waivers" to pay for otherwise uncovered home and community-based services (HCBS) for Medicaid eligible persons who might otherwise be institutionalized. As long as these services are cost-effective, states have few restrictions on the services that may be covered.

Six services may be provided under this program, namely:

- Case management;
- Homemaker/home heath aide services;
- Personal care services;
- Adult day health;
- Rehabilitation; and
- Respite care.

States have the flexibility to design each waiver program and select a combination of waiver services that best meets the needs of the population they wish to serve. HCBS waiver service may be provided statewide or may be limited to specific geographic subdivisions. States may also target specific illnesses, such as children with AIDS.

■ MEDICAID AND MANAGED CARE

States have become increasingly reliant on managed care programs to contain rising Medicaid costs and to improve quality of care. In 1991, only 1 percent of the Medicaid population was enrolled in managed care. By 2000 that figure had risen to 54 percent, or 16.8 million beneficiaries. Forty-eight states and the District of Columbia now operate at least one managed care program.

Medicaid managed care typically means that a state Medicaid program will contract with a private managed care company to provide health care for Medicaid recipients. The promise is that Medicaid recipients are no longer forced to rely on government clinics or the emergency room of a hospital to obtain health care. By placing Medicaid recipients in the private system, they become indistinguishable from privately insured patients.

One of Medicaid's crucial roles as a safety net program is the financing of health services for low-income individuals with disabilities. About one of every six persons on Medicaid can be classified as a "younger" person with a disability—that is, a child or an adult under age 65 who qualifies for Medicaid coverage because of a disability. Because people with disabilities are a costly population to serve, state Medicaid programs have encouraged enrollment of younger persons with disabilities into their managed care programs.

The state managed care programs generally fall into one of two classifications: Primary Care Case Management (PCCM) program and MCO program on a capitated basis.

Primary Care Case Management

Primary Care Case Management is a Medicaid care delivery model that lies between FFS and risk-based managed care. It builds on the standard managed care model by matching beneficiaries with PCPs who coordinate care for the enrollee and who serve as gatekeepers for specialty and other services. Primary care providers who participate in the PCCM program generally receive a monthly management fee, with services paid on a FFS basis. Unlike capitated managed care, the provider is not at financial risk for the services provided.

The advantage of the PCCM program is that beneficiaries with disabilities can benefit from the careful management expected from the PCP. Medicaid beneficiaries consume a sizable share of Medicaid dollars and are frequent users of health services. Any mechanism that can provide better continuity and coordination of care could improve health care for this population.

The disadvantage of the PCCM program is that it restricts choice by placing access to specialists within the purview of the primary care provider/gatekeeper. Another problem is that the beneficiary's previous PCP might not be part of the plan's network of providers. This may require Medicaid beneficiaries to see a new PCP who is unfamiliar with their histories.

Managed Care Organizations on a Capitated Basis

MCOs on a capitated basis is a health care organization (i.e., an HMO) that receives a fixed amount in consideration for making available specified health services to a covered Medicaid beneficiary.

Providing health plans for a lump sum creates incentives to furnish care efficiently and to invest in resources that could prevent costly hospitalizations and emergency room use. This arrangement is intended to promote better disease and disability management and, because the amount received is fixed, there is incentive to use monies more creatively.

On the downside, capitated plans use a network of medical providers, making it likely that some of a beneficiary's previous providers will not be included in the plan. This may cause individuals to sever their relationship with a provider who is not part of the network, creating considerable discontinuity in treatment.

Employment and Medicaid

Many individuals with disability rely on Medicaid coverage that comes with SSI for their health insurance. Given the choice of not working, or working fewer hours, and retaining SSI eligibility and Medicaid versus earning a higher income, becoming SSI ineligible, and losing coverage, most recipients would invariably choose to work fewer hours. To counteract this work disincentive, options have been developed for SSI recipients that provide work incentives and allow recipients to continue their Medicaid eligibility.

Earned Income Exclusion

This program allows a portion of a person's salary to be excluded when figuring the SSI payment amount. Up to $85/month of income has no impact on the SSI check. After that, the check is reduced $1 for every $2 one earns.

For example, Joe Smith earns $553 in earned income.

$ 553	Earned Income
− 85	Disregarded income
$ 468	Divided by 2 = $234 (countable income)
$ 630	SSI benefit (varies by state)
− 234	Income to be deducted
$ 396	Monthly SSI check

Impairment-Related Work Expenses

This incentive allows an SSI recipient to deduct from his/her earnings any disability-related expenses that are necessary to maintaining a job, such as personal care assistance or special transportation costs.

Plan for Achieving Self-Support (PASS)

Under the PASS program, one can save for or set aside SSI or other income for work goals, such as education, vocational training, purchase of adaptive equipment, etc. Plans are reviewed every 12 months.

Section 1619b Continued Medicaid Eligibility

This incentive allows individuals to keep Medicaid insurance even if their earnings become too high to continue receiving SSI benefits. If one needs Medicaid in order to work, Medicaid benefits will continue until the individual's annual income is greater than a state threshold level. In 2001 this threshold level ranged from $16,467 in Arkansas to $34,036 in Arizona.

Ticket to Work and Work Incentives Improvement Act

The Ticket to Work and Work Incentives Improvement Act allows states to make the following changes to Medicaid:

- Expand Medicaid availability to individuals between the ages of 16 and 64 who, because of income earned from work, are ineligible to receive SSI; and
- Extend Medicaid to employed persons with disabilities whose medical condition has improved, but who have continued to have a "severe medically determinable impairment" as defined by the federal Health and Human Services Regulations.

The decision to make these changes to Medicaid is determined by each state. The status of a state's legislation pursuant to this Act can be provided by its Department of Insurance.

Persons in states exercising these options, who previously would not have qualified for Medicaid now:

- Are permitted to buy into Medicaid coverage by paying premiums and other cost-sharing charges on a sliding fee-scale based on income.
- May be required by the state to pay the full premium if their incomes exceed 250 percent of the federal poverty level.
- Are guaranteed that premiums may not exceed 7.5 percent of income if their incomes are between 250 percent and 450 percent of the federal poverty level.

For individuals with annual adjusted gross incomes (as defined by the Internal Revenue Service) exceeding $75,000, states are required to charge 100 percent of the premiums imposed. However, the statute does permit states to subsidize the premium cost for individuals using state funds.

4

SOCIAL SECURITY DISABILITY INSURANCE

Social Security Disability Insurance (SSDI) is an insurance program for workers unable to work due to long-term disability. It is administered by the Social Security Administration (SSA) and funded by a tax (referred to as the FICA tax) withheld from workers' pay and by employer contributions. FICA stands for the Federal Income Contribution Act.

If a person earns enough work "credits," he or she becomes insured for disability benefits. Social Security assigns credits for the amount of earnings that an individual receives and pays taxes on, into the Social Security Trust Fund. Each year the amount of earnings needed to earn one-credit changes. A person can earn up to four credits per year.

The number of work credits needed by an individual for disability benefits depends on when the person becomes disabled. Generally, the applicant needs 20 credits earned in the last 10 years ending with the year when the disability occurs. Younger workers may qualify with fewer hours. The rules are as follows:

- *Before age 24*—An applicant may qualify if he or she has six credits earned in the three-year period ending when the disability starts.
- *Age 24 to 31*—An applicant may qualify if he or she has credit for having worked half the time between age 21 and the outset of the disability. For example, if the individual becomes disabled at age 27, he or she needs credit for three years of work (12 credits) out of the past six years (between ages 21 and 27).
- *Age 31 or older*—In general, the applicant will need to have the number of work credits indicated in the chart shown below. Normally to qualify for SSDI, one needs 40 credits during his or her lifetime (10 years) with 20 of those credits (five years) earned within the last 10 years.

37

Born after 1929, Become Disabled at Age	Credits the Applicant Needs
31 through 42	20
44	22
46	24
48	26
50	28
52	30
54	32
56	34
58	36
60	38
62 or older	40

■ APPLICATION

An individual should apply for SSD when he or she has been out of work or expects to be out of work because of a disability for a period of 12 continuous months. The SSA considers a person disabled if:

- The individual lacks the ability to engage in any substantial gainful activity;
- The incapacity is due to one or more medically determinable physical or mental impairments; and
- The incapacity has lasted or can be expected to last for a continuous period of at least 12 months or to result in death.

The first step in the application process is called the "initial application." It takes between 60 to 90 days just to process the paperwork. An applicant may shorten the process if certain documents are submitted that are needed by SSA to help establish disability. They include:

- Names, addresses, and phone numbers of doctors, therapists, hospitals, clinics, and institutions that treated the applicant, along with the dates of treatment;
- Names of all medications being taken;
- Medical records from doctors, therapists, hospitals, clinics, and caseworkers;
- Letters and reports from at least one doctor based on a recent examination that establishes the diagnosis of the illness or injury that is causing severe interference with work activity, explains the restriction on work capacity resulting from

the diagnosed medical condition, provides examples of what the applicant can and cannot do, and explains if the impairment will either result in death or is expected to last for at least 12 months;
- Laboratory and test results;
- A summary of where the applicant worked or works and the nature of the work; and
- A copy of the individual's W-2 Form or, if self-employed, his or her federal income tax return for the past year.

It is also suggested that the applicant submit at this time a certified copy of his or her birth certificate or other proof of citizenship. As the application process progresses, the candidate may be asked to provide additional information on work history, evidence of military service, proof of military discharge, certified copies of birth certificates of eligible children, workers' compensation award information, and a voided check for direct deposit.

Federal statute provides that the same standard applies in determining disability under both SSDI and SSI. Social Security uses a multi-step process in determining disability including:

- Is the applicant not working or expected not to work;
- Is the applicant engaged in any substantial gainful activity;
- Is the applicant capable of performing relevant work;
- Does the applicant have a severe impairment; and
- Does the applicant have a condition that meets one of Social Security's listed impairments?

A benchmark used by SSA, in the event the applicant is working, is that Social Security does not consider the individual disabled if he or she is working in substantial gainful employment and his or her earnings average more than $780 a month.

It is essential that applicants keep track of their daily activities as part of the application process. They must create a clear mental picture of the problems they face, which in turn must be conveyed to the Social Security representative at the time of application. It is important to convey the symptoms that an individual has on his worst day, not his best day, and to be as comprehensive and descriptive as possible.

■ APPEALS

If an application for SSD benefits is denied (or if earlier approved, having any benefits reduced or terminated), the applicant or recipient is entitled to four opportunities to have that decision reversed. The steps taken include:

1. *After an initial finding is made which is adverse to the claimant, that individual has 60 days to request reconsideration.* The claim is then assigned to an SSA representative who did not participate in the original decision. If the request for reconsideration is made within 10 days of the denial, the claimant's benefits if already in place will continue until the reconsideration is made.
2. *If reconsideration is unsuccessful, the claimant has the right to request a hearing before an administrative law judge (ALJ).* This is similar to a court hearing or trial, but less formal. Testimony is taken under oath and the parties are permitted to submit evidence.
3. *If an adverse decision is rendered, the claimant has the right to request a review by the Social Security Appeals Council in Washington, D.C.* This must be done within 60 days after the date of the determination.
4. The Appeals Council may affirm, modify, or reverse the decision of the ALJ, or may send the case back to the ALJ for further action. Once the Council renders a decision, *the claimant has the right to obtain further review by filing suit within 60 days in a United States District Court.*

According to a ruling on June 5, 2000, by the United States Supreme Court, claimants bringing appeals to the federal district court may now raise additional issues that were not brought up during earlier SSA appeals.

There are two reasons why an SSD applicant should appeal an adverse decision rendered at either the initial finding stage or by the ALJ. First, according to NOSSCR, the National Organization of Social Security Claimant Representatives, 40 percent of the initial applications for SSD are denied. Of those that are rejected, 20 percent are successful at reconsideration and over 50 percent are successful at the disability hearing.

The second reason is due to a policy recently implemented by SSA. If the individual has been unsuccessful at the initial finding stage followed by an adverse ruling rendered by an ALJ (Stage Two), SSA now allows the claimant to file a new SSDI application.

Prior to this change, an applicant had to wait until the Appeals Council ruled on the appeal. According to one commentator, this tribunal generally upheld the ALJ's decision and had a backlog of at least 12 to 15 months between the time the papers were submitted and a decision rendered. During this period, the applicant would be ineligible to receive SSDI benefits or have access to Medicare and was barred from filing a new application.[1]

As an alternative, the applicant could file a new application, but by doing so, would forgo the appeal. This was the recommended course if the claimant had a new

---

[1] *Winning SSDI While You Wait for an Appeal*, About Dot Com, 2000, P.1, http://chronicfatigue.about.com/health/chronicfatigue/library/weekly/aa02600a.htm?rnk=r1&terms=SSDI+Appeals

doctor, attorney, or any new medical evidence that was more persuasive in establishing his or her right to SSDI. However, the problem with starting over was that any rights the applicant had to benefits prior to the new application were lost.

Under the new policy, a subsequent claim will be processed and adjudicated even if there is a prior claim pending at the Appeals Council. This makes it possible for the applicant to be able to win benefits under a new claim even before the appeal on the old one is heard.

If the subsequent application is approved, a favorable outcome might sway the Appeals Council to approve those expenses incurred prior to the second claim and set forth in the initial application. Each case is considered separately and, if the Appeals Council decides that the subsequent claim presents new and material evidence relating to the period prior to the date of the ALJ decision, such new evidence may be used by the Appeal Council's review of the prior claim.[2]

The law provides that disability benefits for workers usually cannot begin for five months after the established onset of the disability. If the beneficiary leaves the disability rolls and returns with the same or a related impairment within five years, Social Security does not require a new waiting period. A beneficiary may also receive SSDI benefits retroactive to one year from the date the application was filed. The five-month waiting period still applies, however.

Should Counsel be Retained During the Application Process?

No one likes to pay attorney fees. This is especially true in an application for Social Security Disability Benefits when the claimant has been diagnosed with a condition that meets one of Social Security's listed impairments. Learning this, the applicant might assume that the application will be swiftly approved after proof of the diagnosis is submitted to the agency. Unfortunately, however, it is not that simple.

SSA requires that an individual be unable to engage in any substantial gainful activity by reason of a medically determinable physical or medical impairment. The condition must be expected to last for a continuous period of not less than 12 months or result in death. Therefore, determination of benefits is based on *functioning*, not on diagnosis. The immediate question is whether the claimant has the skill to present the necessary proof of this impairment to Social Security without legal assistance. And, assuming the applicant possesses this requisite expertise, will there be sufficient control of emotions if his or her integrity is questioned? (For a detailed discussion of these issues, see *Multiple Sclerosis: Your Legal Rights*, Perkins and Perkins, Demos.)

Another factor is the slow pace set by SSA in reaching a decision. For instance, it generally takes at least three to five months for Social Security to gather all the necessary evidence and conduct a hearing before rendering a decision at the initial

---

[2] Id. at P.2

hearing. A skillful attorney knows the roadblocks that are characteristic of the initial application process and how to avoid them.

It is fair to say that every case is different and an attorney's role depends on the particular facts of the case. However, some of the things an attorney may do that can be very time consuming to the novice include:

- Gather medical and other evidence.
- Analyze the case under Social Security Regulations.
- Refer the client to additional doctors whom the attorney has used previously and whose work he or she trusts.
- Send the client to a vocational expert for a report on his or her ability to work.
- Request subpoenas to ensure the presence of crucial witnesses or documents at the hearing.
- Protect the client's right to a fair hearing by objecting to improper evidence and procedures.
- Advise the client how best to prepare himself or herself to testify at the hearing.
- Present a closing statement at the hearing arguing that the client is entitled to benefits under the Social Security Regulations.

An attorney is strongly recommended when an appeal is necessary. Whether one should be retained at the beginning of the application process depends on the expertise and ability of the applicant to negotiate this lengthy and cumbersome process. It is essential that, if an attorney is retained, he or she should be knowledgeable of the SSDI application process and have experience representing individuals pursuing SSDI claims. NOSSCR (National Organization of Social Security Claimant Representatives) is one resource for finding such an attorney.

■ ATTORNEY FEES

Social Security has two methods of authorizing attorney fees: the fee agreement and the fee petition process. Both methods are dependent on the claimant receiving a favorable determination. Therefore, no money is required "up front."

The agreement process requires the claimant and attorney to file a written agreement with the SSA before the date SSA makes a decision on the application. The fee is usually approved if it is limited to 25 percent of past due benefits or $5,300, whichever is less. The fee will be paid only if SSA renders a favorable determination and the claim results in past-due benefits.

A fee greater than $5,300 can only be authorized in cases where the attorney appeals the fee award and files a fee petition. The amount of the fee authorized under the fee petition process is based on several factors including but not limited to:

- The complexity of the case;
- Extent and type of services counsel performed; and
- The amount of time spent by the attorney.

■ TRIAL WORK PERIOD

A person receiving SSD benefits may be entitled to a trial work period depending on his or her medical condition. The period used to determine the individual's ability to work is nine months (to be performed during a 60-month consecutive period) while still drawing the full SSDI monthly benefit. After the nine months of trial work, the beneficiary will lose the SSDI cash benefit if he or she earns more than $780 per month from gainful employment.

■ MEDICARE

Everyone eligible for SSDI also qualifies for Medicare. However, the beneficiary must wait 24 months from the date benefits commence, before coverage becomes effective.

During this qualifying period for Medicare, the recipient might be eligible for health insurance from a former employer or through a program offered by the state where the individual resides.

5

SUPPLEMENTAL SECURITY INCOME

Supplemental Security Income (SSI) is a federal income support program administered by the Social Security Administration (SSA). It is a government benefit that provides a basic monthly income to individuals who are blind, disabled, or 65 years of age or older, and who meet certain financial thresholds. Unlike Social Security Disability Insurance (SSDI), SSI is financed through general tax revenues, not taxes on the earnings of the applicant. Individuals can receive SSI even if they have never worked or would not otherwise qualify for Social Security.

Both disability and financial criteria need to be met in order to be eligible for SSI benefits. The disability must be a medically determinable mental and/or physical condition that is expected to have a duration of a year or longer or to result in death. Financial criteria include earned income (wages) and resource assets (bank accounts and other fluid assets).

Federal statute requires that an SSI applicant reside in the United States, Puerto Rico, or in the Northern Marina Islands, the U.S. Virgin Islands, or Guam; be a United States citizen or permanent resident with 40 work credits; be either a recipient or applicant of Social Security benefits (if eligible); and, if disabled, be a participant in a vocational rehabilitation program, assuming that one is offered. If an applicant is receiving Social Security benefits, there is no rule that would prohibit the individual from receiving SSI as well.

■ FINANCIAL ELIGIBILITY

An individual applying to receive SSI cannot have assets that exceed $2,000. For a couple, the assets cannot have a value in excess of $3,000, even if only one individual is eligible for such benefits. In addition, an applicant's earned income may not be over $780 per month.

Certain assets are not included in determining SSI eligibility. They are:

- The family home;
- One automobile;
- Burial plots for an individual applicant and his or her immediate family;
- Burial funds up to $1,500; and
- Life insurance with a face value of $1,500 or less.

Under SSI, income may be derived from cash or checks (their inclusion being dependent on the source of payment), as well as an array of assets (some of which may not even be reported on federal, state, or local income tax returns). Examples include:

- Wages from work, whether in cash or in another form;
- Net earnings from a business if the applicant is self-employed;
- The value of food, clothing, or shelter that someone gives the applicant, or the amount of money given to that individual to help pay for such items;
- Department of Veterans Affairs (VA) benefits;
- Social Security benefits;
- Annuities, pensions, workers' compensation, and unemployment insurance benefits;
- Proceeds from life insurance policies;
- Gifts and contributions;
- Child support and alimony; and
- Inheritance in cash or property.

The following items are not considered income:

- Medical care and services;
- Social Services;
- Receipts from the sale, exchange, or replacement of assets owned by the applicant;
- Income tax refunds;
- Earned income tax credit payments and proceeds of a loan;
- Bills paid by someone else for items other than food, clothing, or shelter;
- Replacement of lost or stolen income;
- Home energy assistance;
- The first $20 of most income received in a month;

- The first $65 earned by the applicant from working and half the amount over $65; and
- Food stamps.

■ APPLICATION

Once a decision has been made to apply for SSI benefits, the first step is to telephone SSA to schedule an appointment. The toll free number is 800-772-1213. Representatives are available from 7:00 AM to 7:00 PM each business day.

At the time of the first appointment, the SSA representative attending the meeting will request a number of documents. The more documentation the applicant has in advance, the more efficient the application process. Some of the items most likely to be requested at this meeting include:

- Social Security card;
- Proof of age, which may be documented by either the original or certified copy of the applicant's birth certificate;
- Proof of resources consisting of bank accounts, life insurance, cash, etc.;
- Proof of income, paycheck stubs, or copies of payment received;
- Proof of living arrangements, rent, or mortgage payments;
- Names, addresses, and telephone numbers of doctors, hospitals, and clinics; and
- Documentation from employers, preferably by means of notarized statements, detailing work limitations due to the disability.

Applications may also be submitted by an authorized representative, but must also be signed by the applicant unless that individual is under the age of 18, is not physically able to sign, or lacks the mental competence to do so. In these cases, a court appointed representative or other responsible person may sign on the applicant's behalf.

■ DISABILITY DETERMINATION

Federal statute provides that the same standard applies in determining disability for SSI and SSDI. Social Security uses a multi-step process in reaching this determination and includes the following factors:

- Is the applicant not working or expected not to work?
- Is the applicant engaged in any substantial gainful activity?

- Is the applicant capable of performing relevant work?
- Does the applicant have a severe impairment?
- Does the applicant have a condition that meets one of Social Security's listed impairments?

The paperwork is the same as that required for someone establishing a disability when applying for SSDI benefits. The doctor's report, based on a recent examination, should include:

1. Establishing a diagnosis of the illness or injury that is causing severe impairment of the work activity.
2. Explaining the restriction of work capacity resulting from the diagnosed medical condition.
3. Providing examples of what the patient can and cannot do.
4. Explaining whether the impairment will either result in death or is expected to last at least 12 months.

The applicant must be unable to engage in any substantial activity by reason of a medically determinable physical or mental impairment that is expected to last for a continuous period of not less than 12 months or result in death.

■ APPEAL

If the SSA denies the initial application for SSI, the applicant has the right to appeal the denial of the claim. The four stages of the appeal are:

- Reconsideration
- Administrative law judge (ALJ) hearing
- Appeals council review
- Federal court appeal

The claimant has 60 days from the time he or she receives a denial of the application to appeal the decision. Failure to file a timely appeal may result in a waiver of his or her rights for SSI benefits. An attorney may be retained at any level of the decision making process.

It is not unusual for an initial application to be rejected. In Minnesota, for example, a recent study indicated that 60 percent of the original applications were denied. Many of these initial denials were overturned when appealed. Reconsideration is the first level of appeal. The reversal rate at this level was approximately 14 percent. The reversal rate was 60 percent when denials were appealed at the next level, which was before the ALJ. It is essential for a client applying for SSI (or SSDI) to know these statistics, because the process is lengthy and rejection notices disheartening when issued without what appears to be a consideration of the facts supporting the disability.

If the application is approved, the amount of the monthly SSI benefit is dependent on the recipient's income and living arrangements. For instance, in the year 2002, the maximum monthly amount paid by the federal government to an individual is $545. The maximum amount paid to a couple is $817. In addition, 43 states provide supplemental payments to beneficiaries.

■ MEDICAID COVERAGE

SSI beneficiaries are automatically eligible for Medicaid in 38 states. The other states have more restricted standards of eligibility.

Medicaid is a jointly funded federal–state health insurance program for low-income and needy people. It covers children, the aged, the blind, and/or the disabled and other people eligible to receive federally assisted income maintenance payments. The Center for Medicare and Medicaid Services oversees state administration of Medicaid. Title XIX of the Social Security Act authorizes Medicaid.

Thirty-two states and the District of Columbia authorize Medicaid eligibility to people eligible for SSI benefits. In these states, your SSI application is also your Medicaid application.

The following states use the same rules to decide eligibility for Medicaid as are used for SSI, but require the claimant to file a separate application:

Alaska	Nebraska	Utah
Idaho	Nevada	Northern Marina Islands
Kansas	Oregon	

The following states have their own eligibility criteria for Medicaid, which are different from the SSI rules. In these states, a claimant will have to file a separate application for Medicaid:

Connecticut	Minnesota	Ohio
Hawaii	Missouri	Oklahoma
Illinois	North Dakota	New Hampshire
Indiana		Virginia

Once an SSI and/or Medicaid application is approved, Medicaid coverage will become effective immediately. There is no premium charged for coverage.

Should Counsel be Retained During the Application Process?

As noted earlier for SSD benefits, no one likes to pay attorney fees. An individual might assume that the application will be swiftly approved after proof of diagnosis is submitted to SSA. Unfortunately, however, it is not that simple. SSA requires that an individual's condition has progressed to the point that he or she is functionally unable to engage in substantial gainful activity. Determination of benefits is based on functioning, not diagnosis. As for SSD benefits, the condition must be expected to last for a continuous period of not less than 12 months or to result in death to qualify. A person who wants to represent him- or herself must be confident that he or she has the skills to present the necessary proof to Social Security. Assuming that the applicant possesses the requisite expertise, will there be sufficient control of emotions if his or her integrity is questioned?

Another factor to consider is the slow pace set by SSA in reaching a decision. For example, it generally takes three to five months for Social Security to gather all the necessary evidence and conduct a hearing before rendering a decision. A skillful attorney knows the roadblocks that are characteristic of the initial application process and how to avoid them.

It is fair to say that every case is different and an attorney's role depends on the particular facts of the case. However, some of the things an attorney may do that can be very time consuming to the novice include:

- Gather medical and other evidence;
- Analyze the case under the Social Security regulations;
- Refer the client to additional doctors whom the attorney has used previously and whose work he or she trusts;
- Send the client to a vocational expert for a report on his or her ability to work; and
- Request subpoenas to ensure the presence of crucial witnesses or documents at the hearing.

In conclusion, an attorney is strongly recommended when an appeal is necessary. Whether one should be retained at the beginning of the application process depends on the ability and expertise of the applicant to negotiate this lengthy and cumbersome process. It is essential that, if an attorney is retained, he or she should be knowledgeable of the SSI application process and preferably have experience representing individuals pursuing such claims previously. As with SSD benefits, NOSSCR is one resource for finding such an attorney.

■ ATTORNEY FEES

An attorney may charge and receive a fee for his or her services, but the SSA decides how much the fee will be. Generally, the maximum fee that will be authorized is 25 percent of the retroactive payment or $5,300, whichever is less. A representative cannot charge or receive more than the fee amount authorized. SSI differs from SSDI in that amounts cannot be withheld from an individual's SSI benefits to pay for attorney fees. SSI claimants are responsible for paying such fees directly to their attorneys.

6

SSDI/SSI: THE APPLICATION PROCESS

Once someone has reached a decision to apply for SSDI or SSI, his or her first step is to telephone the SSA at 800-772-1213 between the hours of 7:00 AM and 7:00 PM Eastern Standard Time and request the following:

- The pamphlet entitled *Disability Benefits*
- Social Security Application
- Earnings and Benefits Estimate Statement

The person applying for SSDI or SSI needs to be aware that the procedure is not easy. This includes awareness that the process could take between six to eight months and requires the submission of a large amount of paperwork that will establish, among other things, proof of a disability and the applicant's work history.

Although there is no hard rule that the applicant must quit working before applying for benefits, any work is considered a factor by the SSA in establishing the presence of a disability. However, an application will be denied if the individual is earning more than $780 per month in substantial gainful employment.

■ STEP 1: DESCRIPTION OF DISABILITY

This step can be started before the application is received. In order to prepare for completing the SSDI/SSI application when it arrives, it is recommended that the applicant maintain, for at least one week, a log of daily activities that records the occurrence of symptoms, such as the following:

- Visual difficulties
- Tremors
- Balance problems
- Memory loss
- Speech difficulties
- Weakness
- Bladder control
- Emotional distress
- Spasms
- Fatigue
- Sexual difficulties
- Numbness
- Cognitive problems

It is also essential that the applicant keep track of his or her daily activities to help create a clear mental picture of the problems he or she faces, which in turn must be conveyed to the Social Security representative at the time of application. It is important to convey symptoms an individual has on one's worst day, not one's best day, and to be as comprehensive and descriptive as possible.

Following is a suggested self-survey containing the types of questions that need to be answered in the application for SSDI/SSI. The Application for Disability Insurance Benefits and Disability Report forms can be obtained from the SSA Web site—www.ssa.gov.

Self-Survey to be Answered in Preparation for Applying for SSDI or SSI

Name: _____

Date of Diagnosis: _____

I. GETTING OUT OF BED

1. How long does it take you to get up in the morning?
2. Do you require assistance to get up?
3. Once you are standing do you hold onto anything to steady yourself?
4. When walking to the bathroom, do you touch the walls? (This is called *wall walking*.) Why?

II. PERSONAL HYGIENE

1. If male, do you sit to urinate?
2. To shower, do you need assistance to get into the shower?
3. Do you sit or stand while showering?
4. If you stand while showering, do you lean against the shower wall?
5. Have you ever needed assistance in bathing?
6. Have you ever burned yourself because of the water temperature?
7. After you finish bathing, do you pause before you exit? How long?
8. Do you sit on the toilet seat to rest before you exit the bathroom?
9. To return to your room, do you use the walls for assistance?

III. DRESSING

1. Do you require assistance in selecting your clothes?
2. Do you dress in stages? For example, do you put on your shirt, and then pause before you select the next article of clothing?
3. Do you need assistance with buttons, snaps, or shoestrings?
4. Why do you need this assistance?
5. Do you need to rest after dressing? How long is this rest period?
6. How long does the entire dressing process take?

IV. MEAL PREPARATION

1. Has there been a change in the amount of food preparation that you can do independently?
2. What do you usually have for breakfast, lunch, and dinner?
3. Who prepares or assists you with meal preparation?
4. Why do you need assistance?
5. Have you ever fallen while preparing a meal?
6. Do dishes or pots and pans fall from your hands without warning?
7. Have you ever scalded yourself while making a meal?
8. Do you ever skip meals because you are too tired to prepare the food yourself?
9. Have you ever set off the smoke alarm because you forgot something on the stove?
10. Who does the shopping?

V. HOUSEHOLD DUTIES

1. Do you do your own personal shopping?
2. If not, who assists you?
3. Do you pay your own bills?
4. Do you take care of your banking needs?
5. Do you do your own laundry?
6. Do you drive?
7. Who assists you in your transportation needs?
8. Do you consider yourself a safe driver?
9. Who cleans your house?

VI. RECREATIONAL/SOCIAL

1. Before your symptoms began, what were your hobbies?
2. Have these hobbies changed?
3. What do you now do for entertainment?
4. How often do you visit your friends and family?
5. How often do friends and family come to visit you?
6. If you are a parent, how active are you with the children?
7. Has your interaction with the children changed?

You have explored your activities of daily living in great detail through this log. If there is any additional information you feel is important, that has not been addressed, please list it:

1. _____
   _____
   _____

2. _____
   _____
   _____

3. _____
   _____
   _____

■ STEP 2: WORK HISTORY

1. List the jobs held for the past 15 years:

Job title	Kind of business	Dates worked
_____	_____	_____
_____	_____	_____
_____	_____	_____

2. List basic duties of these jobs.
3. List any machines/tools or equipment you can use.
4. List any technical knowledge you may have.
5. Have you had supervisory responsibilities?

   Which do you do more of and how much of each in hours per day?
   Sitting _____
   Standing _____
   Walking _____
   (Note: The total of these three activities need to amount to eight hours.)

■ STEP 3: PHYSICIAN CONTACTS

Assemble the names and addresses, zip codes, and phone numbers of all the doctors and allied health professionals you have seen or who have treated you for your condition and/or its symptoms. Your list may include your:

- Neurologist or other medical specialist
- General practitioner
- Neuro-opthalmologist
- Urologist
- Physiatrist
- Psychiatric psychologist
- OT/PT

■ STEP 4: FILING APPLICATION

Once the application packet is received from the Social Security Office:

1. Complete all forms as required.

2. Contact all doctors who have treated you to let them know that they will be requested to send your records to the Social Security Office. You may also want to request a copy of these records for yourself. The submission of the doctor's report should be based on a recent examination and include:
   - Establishing the diagnosis of the illness or injury that is causing severe impairment of the work activity;
   - Explaining the restriction on work capacity resulting from the diagnosed medical condition;
   - Providing examples of what you can and cannot do; and
   - Explaining if the impairment will either result in death or is expected to last at least 12 months.

7

EMPLOYEE RETIREMENT INCOME SECURITY ACT

In 1974, the federal government passed the Employee Retirement Income Security Act (ERISA) for the purpose of establishing uniform federal standards for pension and employee benefit plans, including health insurance plans. The primary purpose of adopting ERISA was to protect the solvency and security of employee pension plans. However, because the statute contained language pre-empting all state laws related to employee benefit plans, which could include health insurance plans, an unintended benefit was given to employers regarding health plans funded entirely by them (referred to as a "self-funded plan").

In a self-funded plan, the employer, not an insurance company, collects all the premiums and pays out all the benefits. The employer is not purchasing a plan from an insurance company, but administering the plan itself. By doing so, it does not need to pay the administrative and overhead costs to the insurance company, nor is it regulated by state insurance regulations. On the other hand, it assumes all the risks of the plan.

■ ERISA PRE-EMPTION

If an employer purchases a health insurance plan from a licensed insurance company, the insurer must comply with all applicable state insurance requirements. However, if the plan is funded entirely by the employer, ERISA pre-empts regulators from imposing such requirements on the employer. In other words, state legislatures and insurance regulators have the authority to impose requirements on insurers. ERISA pre-empts them from imposing health benefit plan requirements on employers.

The lack of state regulation limits the options available to those seeking accountability for medical decisions that resulted in harm—even if those decisions contradict the recommendation of the treating physician. Under ERISA, the family of a patient who is injured or dies as a result of a health plan decision can only recover the cost of a denied benefit. ERISA prevents the family or patient from holding the plan accountable for the pain and suffering caused by the negligence.

Erosion of the ERISA Pre-emption

Since the mid-1990s, ERISA's pre-emption of state laws has weakened. In the courts, the change began with a 1995 United States Supreme Court case, *New York State Conference of Blue Cross and Blue Shield versus Travelers Insurance Co.*, which held that New York could apply surcharges to the hospital bills of patients insured under self-funded plans. The decision represented the first major pullback by the Supreme Court from its longstanding reluctance to interpret the ERISA pre-emption standard expansively.

A more dramatic example of this turnaround can be found in a 1999 case decided by a federal district court. In this action, the insurer, an HMO, denied the plaintiff's teenage son psychiatric care, although he had tried to commit suicide on two occasions within a month. A week later, the boy committed suicide and the parents sued the HMO. Although the defendant raised ERISA as a defense, the court held that the claim fell outside the jurisdiction of ERISA because it involved medical negligence, not the improper denial of medical benefits. Earlier, this defense would have almost certainly been sufficient to dismiss the suit.

On the federal legislative level, there has also been action to eliminate the ERISA pre-emption. In 1999, the U.S. House of Representatives approved the Norwood-Dingle bill, which would have permitted patients to hold managed care insurers legally accountable for the delay or denial of care that resulted in injury or death. Although the Senate adopted a much weaker bill and the two houses were unable to reach a compromise on the legislation, politically it appears that a measure could be adopted that eliminates or at the very least weakens the pre-emption defense.

States have also been active in eliminating the ERISA pre-emption. In May 1997, Texas became the first state in which managed care organizations (MCOs) could be sued directly for medical malpractice. The law was challenged in federal court, but in September 1998, a decision was rendered holding that the right-to-sue portion of the statute was valid.

During 1998, 29 states debated proposals that would have permitted plan members to sue their MCOs for medical malpractice. Although none of these states enacted legislation removing this ban, New Mexico adopted a bill permitting patients to sue their health plans for violation of the state's Patient Protection Act.

The New Mexico statute provides that the state Department of Insurance must draft regulations requiring at a minimum that MCOs (1) provide health care services that are "reasonably accessible and available in a timely manner;" (2) offer a sufficient number of health care providers; and (3) establish prompt and fair grievance procedures. Unlike the Texas Act, which establishes a cause of action for medical malpractice, the New Mexico law limits the plan member's right to sue to those occasions when there have been violations to one of the state's patient protection measures.

Another example of how federal pre-emption is being weakened is in the stand now being taken by the United States Department of Labor. The Department of Labor's Pension and Welfare Benefits Administration regulates ERISA. Recently, the Department of Labor has taken an active role in limiting the scope of ERISA by filing "friend of the court briefs" in litigation, challenging the dominance of the pre-emption defense. This is especially true in the area of medical malpractice, when HMOs have attempted to avoid state-based malpractice actions on the assertion that they are exempt from state regulations because they are ERISA plans. Officials of the Department of Labor state that their efforts in these matters have succeeded.

On June 12, 2000, the United States Supreme Court issued one of its most important decisions regarding ERISA protections and exemptions. In the case of *Pegram versus Herdrich*, Mrs. Herdrich claimed that the decision by her HMO physician, Dr. Pegram, to delay her medical treatment, which resulted in a burst appendix, was driven by the self-interest of the physician to increase her HMO incentive bonuses, therefore violating her fiduciary duty under ERISA. (ERISA defines a fiduciary as one who administers the plan and acts solely in the interest of the plan's participants and beneficiaries). If the court agreed that HMO decisions are "fiduciary acts," Dr. Pegram's failure to act causing medical harm could be viewed as a breach of fiduciary duty, and would allow the plaintiff to seek monetary damages in federal court.

The Supreme Court held that decisions made by plan doctors are not fiduciary acts within the meaning of ERISA. ERISA focuses on eligibility and benefit coverage, and is not intended to govern medical treatment issues. Therefore, "treatment" decisions made by doctors that lead to claims of medical negligence do not come under federal law. Instead, state law should provide the insured with the appropriate remedies to hold HMOs accountable.

The importance of this decision is that it upholds the view that HMOs must be held accountable for harm to patients. Although not an issue for federal court, referring to applicable state law opens the way for expanded state legislation and regulation of ERISA plans.

On November 22, 2000, the Department of Labor issued final regulations in response to President Clinton's memorandum of February 20, 1998, directing the Secretary of Labor to issue regulations strengthening the internal appeals process for ERISA health plans. The final rule, which became effective on January 1, 2002, requires ERISA plans to abide by strict deadlines in notifying patients about coverage. They now have 72 hours to tell patients whether treatments in potentially life-threatening situations are covered, and 15 days to disclose the coverage for non-urgent care.

The new regulations also provide:

- More time for the insured to appeal denied health claims;
- More information about the reasons for the denied claim and the criteria and rules applied by the plan;
- Different decision makers to handle the initial determination and review of the decision; and
- Timely action for claimants receiving a course of treatment who face an early termination of benefits or have a need to extend treatment.

Finally, on June 20, 2002, a divided (5–4) U.S. Supreme Court ruled in the case of *Rush Prudential HMO, Inc. versus Moran*, that the Illinois Health Maintenance Organization Act is not pre-empted by ERISA. In this case, Moran had sought independent treatment review after her HMO denied coverage for surgery. The HMO was a self-insured plan regulated by ERISA, which does not require independent treatment review. The Illinois Act provides for independent medical review of certain denials for service, including disputes between the primary physician and the HMO regarding medical necessity. In deciding this case, the court did not find any congressional intent for ERISA to preclude the Illinois statute and its application to the HMO.

Patient protection advocates have reason to hope for broad-reaching application of this decision. It could influence congressional debate of federal patient protection legislation that would extend protections, including access to independent review, to all ERISA self-insured health plans.

8

HEALTH INSURANCE PORTABILITY AND ACCOUNTABILITY ACT

The Health Insurance Portability and Accountability Act of 1996 (HIPAA), also known as the Kassebaum-Kennedy Bill, is legislation that mandates extensive new requirements for "group health plans." The law is intended to reduce barriers by guaranteeing that most workers who change or lose jobs will have access to health insurance coverage. The act extends to all group health plans (whether insured or self-funded) covering employees, former employees, self-employed individuals, and those (including their dependents) who are associated or formerly associated with the employer in a business relationship. The coverage includes medical, dental, vision, prescription drugs, flexible spending accounts, and some employee assistance plans.

However, the legislation does not extend to group health plans that cover fewer than two participants, guarantee access to health insurance for those who do not have health coverage, nor regulate premium rates.

■ GUARANTEED PROTECTIONS

HIPAA protects participants and their families by:

- Limiting exclusions for pre-existing medical conditions that previously locked workers into jobs or prevented individuals from starting their own businesses for fear of losing health coverage;
- Prohibiting discrimination on the basis of a person's health status, including the premiums charged for someone with a pre-existing condition;

- Guaranteeing availability and renewability of health coverage;
- Preserving the states' role in regulating health insurance, including its authority to provide greater protection;
- Modifying COBRA health care continuation rules; and
- Requiring provisions to reduce health care fraud and abuse.

■ PRE-EXISTING CONDITION

In an effort to increase health care portability, the 1996 Act limits the ability of "group health plans" to exclude individuals from coverage based on the presence of a "pre-existing condition." Under the law, a pre-existing condition will be covered without a waiting period when one joins a new group plan if he or she had been insured the previous 12 months. If that individual has not been insured during the previous 12 months before joining the plan, the longest he or she will have to wait before being covered for the condition is 12 months (or in the case of a late enrollee, 18 months). Once the 12-month period has expired, no new pre-existing condition limit may again be imposed unless there is a gap in coverage of more than 63 days.

A pre-existing condition is defined as a medical condition that was diagnosed or treated in the six-month period preceding the enrollment date of the new plan. For example, if an individual was diagnosed with multiple sclerosis two years before the enrollment date in a new plan and was not treated within six months of that date. MS would not be viewed as a pre-existing condition. If, however, that same individual had been treated for MS during the six months preceding the enrollment date, it would be considered a pre-existing condition. It should be noted that medication is considered treatment under the six-month look-back rule.

HIPAA provides that group health plans have to reduce any pre-existing conditions' exclusion period by the length of time a person had prior coverage. However, plans are not required to take into account any days of creditable coverage that precedes a break in coverage of 63 days or more. State law might extend this period.

HIPAA also applies to insurance sold outside the employer group market. In order to be guaranteed access to individual health coverage, the applicant must:

- Have at least 18 months of aggregate creditable coverage;
- Have been covered under a group health plan, a governmental plan, or a church plan (or health insurance offered in connection with such plans) during the most recent period of creditable coverage;
- Not be eligible for coverage under a group health plan, Medicare, or Medicaid;
- Not have other health insurance coverage;

- Not have had recent coverage canceled for non-payment of premiums or fraud; and
- Have elected and exhausted any option for continuation of coverage (coverage under COBRA or similar state law) that was available under the prior plan.

A person meeting these conditions is considered to be an "eligible individual," which means that he or she must be allowed to procure individual health coverage with no pre-existing condition exclusion.

■ NON-DISCRIMINATION BASED ON HEALTH STATUS

The practical impact of establishing these guidelines on pre-existing conditions is that no enrollment may be delayed or otherwise conditioned upon a health-related factor. Health status-related factors include medical condition, claims experience, receipt of medical care, medical history, genetic information, and evidence of insurability. This would prohibit the practice of requiring an individual to furnish satisfactory evidence of good health as a condition of enrolling in a plan.

This guideline also blocks delaying the effective date of coverage (or the effective date of changes in coverage) due to the individual's confinement in a hospital or failure to be "actively at work" because of illness, injury, or a leave of absence that is medically related.

In addition, HIPAA prohibits discrimination with regard to the amounts charged for premiums. Under the statute, a group health plan may not charge an individual, as a condition of enrollment or continued enrollment in the plan, a premium or contribution that is greater than the premium or contribution that would be paid by a similarly situated individual enrolled in the plan, based on a health related factor. However, the statute does not preclude a group health plan from reducing premiums, co-payments, or deductibles in exchange for an individual's compliance with a bona-fide wellness program (i.e., health promotion and/or disease prevention programs.)

■ CERTIFICATE OF COVERAGE

In order to ensure that a new plan or insurer will recognize an individual's prior health coverage, HIPAA requires the issuance of a Certificate of Coverage. The Certificate enables an individual to provide evidence of creditable coverage in order to reduce or completely avoid any pre-existing condition exclusion that would otherwise limit the coverage of a subsequent group or individual health plan.

Legislation requires that plans and issuers must furnish the certificates automatically to:

- An individual entitled to elect COBRA continuation coverage, at a time no later than when a notice is required to be provided for a qualifying event under COBRA (see Chapter 9 for a detailed explanation of COBRA);
- An individual who loses coverage under a group health plan and who is not entitled to elect COBRA continuation coverage, within a reasonable time after coverage ceases; and
- An individual who has elected COBRA continuation coverage, either within a reasonable time after a plan learns that COBRA continuation coverage ceased or, if applicable, within a reasonable time after the individual's grace period for the payment of COBRA premiums ends.

If the insured has more than 18 months of uninterrupted coverage, the certificate may simply show 18 months of creditable coverage without mentioning dates. If coverage is less than 18 months, the certificate must disclose the dates coverage commenced and ended. In any case, the certificate needs only to disclose the most recent period of continuous coverage without a 63-day break in coverage.

A certificate must also be furnished at the written request of the participant, the covered spouse, or any of the insured dependents, providing the request is made within 24 months after coverage ceases under the plan. When a certificate is requested, it must disclose each period of continuous coverage.

■ MODIFICATION OF EMPLOYEE RETIREMENT INCOME SECURITY ACT (ERISA) PRE-EMPTION

Although ERISA's broad pre-emption of state insurance laws continues to apply for self-insured plans, HIPAA excludes certain categories of state law from pre-emption. Some of the more prominent examples include:

- State insurance laws that limit the pre-existing look-back period to less than six months;
- State insurance laws that impose a shorter pre-existing exclusion period than the ones mandated by HIPAA (i.e., less than 12 months);
- State insurance laws that require that a significant break in coverage be greater than 63 consecutive days; and
- State insurance laws that bar the application of a pre-existing exclusion period to situations other than pregnancy and certain children enrolled within 30 days.

■ MODIFICATIONS TO COBRA

HIPAA also made some modifications to COBRA.

COBRA allows employees to continue health coverage at their own expense for 18 months if they are (1) temporarily or permanently laid off, (2) if their hours are reduced, or (3) who are otherwise severed from employment. The 1996 Act extends COBRA benefits to individuals who become disabled at any time during the first 60 days of COBRA continuation—rather than disabled only at the time of employment termination or reduction of hours. In this instance, the individual is entitled to up to 29 months of coverage. During the first 18 months of coverage, the insurer may not charge more than 102 percent of the applicable premium. For the remaining 11 months of coverage, the insurer may ask up to 150 percent of the premium charged the employer.

It should be observed that COBRA continuation coverage might be terminated if a qualified beneficiary becomes covered under another group health plan and that plan contains no pre-existing condition limitations.

■ LONG-TERM CARE INSURANCE

The tax consequences of long-term care insurance have also been modified under HIPAA. The new provision ensures that the tax treatment for private long-term care insurance is the same as for major medical coverage.

Once a plan becomes tax-qualified, the taxpayer may claim "qualified long-term care insurance premiums" and unreimbursed long-term care medical expenses as itemized medical deductions on Schedule A, Form 1040, if this figure, along with other deductible medical expenses, exceeds 7.5 percent of the adjusted gross income.

To benefit under the policy, the individual claiming these long-term expenses must be chronically ill, which is defined as being (1) unable to perform at least two activities of daily living (i.e., eating, toileting, continence) without special assistance from another person for a period of at least 90 days; or (2) requiring substantial supervision to protect that individual from threats to health and safety due to severe cognitive impairment. A health care practitioner is the one called upon to make this determination.

The expenses that qualify for tax deduction include monies expended on necessary diagnostic, preventive, therapeutic, curing, and rehabilitative services.

■ MEDICAL SAVINGS ACCOUNT

HIPAA also introduced the medical savings account (MSA), which became effective on January 1, 1997.

The MSAs are an approach to controlling health care costs by placing more responsibility on consumers. In most instances, an MSA would be established for and owned by the employee, with funds provided by the employer. The employee would draw on the funds to pay for unreimbursed medical expenses.

As long as the money is withdrawn for qualified medical expenses, the distributions are tax-free. Qualified medical expenses are those deductions allowed on Schedule A of the individual federal income tax return (1040). With an MSA, however, the taxpayer may pay medical bills with pre-tax dollars.

Congress established MSAs as a demonstration program to enable the Government Accounting Office (GAO) to evaluate these accounts and assess their impact on conventional insurance and health care costs. To date, lack of utilization has prevented the GAO from fully conducting this study. A proposal is under consideration in Congress to extend this MSA demonstration from 2002 to 2004.

■ HEALTH CARE FRAUD

A major issue addressed by HIPAA was the adoption of measures designed to fight health care fraud. Demonstrating its commitment, Congress appropriated $104 million in 1997 to carry out its agenda, with increases in increments of 15 percent per year to 2003. Some of the major features of the health care fraud section of HIPAA include:

- The strengthening of the mandate given to the Office of Inspector General (OIG), the FBI, and the Department of Justice to enable those agencies to investigate all health care fraud, regardless of the source of payment. In addition, the Department of Justice is given the authority to subpoena records relating to health care fraud regardless of the payer source.

- The enactment of the crime of "health care fraud," making it illegal for anyone to "knowingly and willfully execute a scheme to defraud any health care benefit program, in connection with the delivery of or payment for health care benefits, or to obtain, by means of false representations, any of the property of a health care benefit program." The crime is premised on the existing statutory provisions of mail and wire fraud, although the penalties under the health care fraud section are more extensive and the crime is targeted to the health care business. The crime does not require use of the U.S. mail or interstate wire system, but instead involves any efforts to defraud health care payers, no matter how the fraud is conducted.

- The creation of the Medicare Integrity Program, through which the Secretary of Health and Human Services will enter into contracts with private sector concerns to carry out Medicare investigative activities.

- The establishment of a program designed to encourage Medicare beneficiaries to report fraud and authorizing the payment of rewards for furnishing information.
- The creation of a department in the OIG given the authority to issue advisory opinions on the permissibility of certain business plans.
- The enactment of a new civil money penalty that imposes fines against physicians who falsely certify home health care for individuals not requiring the same.
- The creation of a database to maintain information on providers that have been sanctioned for health care fraud and abuse. The database is limited to "final adverse actions," a phrase that specifically excludes "settlements in which no finding of liability have been made."
- The enactment of a new crime for the obstruction of investigations involving federal health care offenses. It applies to any health care investigation and process by a criminal investigator, which means any health care fraud investigator for a prosecutorial agency.

■ PRIVACY

HIPAA legislation also establishes privacy rules to give individuals more control over their health information. It requires health plans and providers to have written privacy procedures, to train employees involved in handling protected information, and to establish a grievance procedure. Providers with direct treatment relationships are required to make a good faith effort to obtain an individual's written acknowledgment that he or she is aware of the provider's privacy practices.

■ SUMMARY

As should be readily seen, the Kassebaum-Kennedy Act changed the face of health insurance for individuals with pre-existing conditions. Although portability does not mean that people will carry the same health insurance plan from job to job, it does mean that individuals with pre-existing conditions will not lose coverage because of a change in jobs (assuming that the new employer provides coverage) or health plans. It also addresses an issue requiring the nation's immediate attention, namely health care fraud.

The practical impact on establishing the guidelines on pre-existing condition is that no enrollment may be delayed or otherwise conditioned upon a health-related factor. This would prohibit the earlier practice of requiring a new employee to furnish satisfactory evidence of good health as a condition to enroll in the employer's plan. Health-related factors include medical condition, claims experience, receipt of medical care, medical history, genetic information, and evidence of insurability.

9

CONSOLIDATED OMNIBUS BUDGET RECONCILIATION ACT OF 1985

In 1985, the United States Congress enacted legislation, commonly referred to as COBRA (the Consolidated Omnibus Budget Reconciliation Act) to provide a vital health plan bridge for qualified workers and their spouses and dependent children who might otherwise lose their health insurance coverage. Its security and breadth is seen as a much-needed safety net for families in the midst of crises such as unemployment, divorce, or death.

COBRA requires employers that offer group health coverage to their employees to provide a continuation of the insurance, which would have otherwise been lost due to a termination of employment. Premiums are paid by the former employee, but at the employer's group rate, not as an individual policy. COBRA generally covers health plans of employers who have 20 or more employees working at least 50 percent of the days in the previous calendar year. When used in this context, the term "employee" includes individuals working full-time and part-time, as well as those who are self-employed, provided they are eligible to participate in the employer health plan on the day before a "qualifying event."

The coverage is broad, applying to plans in both the private sector and those established for individuals employed by state and local government. The federal government and certain church-related organizations are not subject to COBRA.

As to those employers subject to the statute, COBRA benefits have to be provided to employees benefiting from coverage and to their spouses and dependents covered under the plan. However, the law stipulates that COBRA does not extend to the following individuals:

- An employee who is not yet eligible for the employer's group health plan (e.g., a new or part-time employee).
- An employee whose employment was terminated due to gross misconduct.
- An eligible employee who declines coverage.
- An individual who is enrolled for benefits under Medicare.

■ QUALIFYING EVENTS

The continuation of insurance coverage, which is at the heart of COBRA, is determined by what is called a qualifying event—an occurrence that triggers the insured's protection under COBRA, requiring the continuation of benefits under a group insurance plan for former employees and their families who would otherwise lose health care coverage. Whether a circumstance is defined as a qualifying event is contingent on the status of the insured. The rules are also dependent on whether the insured is the employee, the spouse of the employee, or his or her dependent.

The qualifying events for employees are:

- Voluntary or involuntary termination of employment for reasons other than "gross misconduct" and
- A reduction in the number of hours, thus changing the status of the insured to part-time, thereby eliminating his or her eligibility.

The qualifying events for spouses are:

- Voluntary or involuntary termination of the covered employee's employment for any reasons other than "gross misconduct";
- A reduction in the number of hours worked by the covered employee;
- Covered employees becoming entitled to Medicare;
- Divorce or legal separation of the covered employee; and
- Death of the covered employee.

The qualifying events for *dependent children* are the same as for the spouse with the following addition:

- Loss of dependent child status under the plan rules.

Depending upon the type of event and who the beneficiary is, coverage could continue for 18, 29, or 36 months after the date of the event of the coverage loss. The law provides as follows:

Qualifying Events	Beneficiary	Coverage
Termination	Employee	18 months[1]
Reduced hours	Spouse Dependent child	
Employee enrolled in Medicare and divorce, legal separation, or death of a covered employee	Spouse Dependent child	36 months
Loss of dependent child status	Dependent child	36 months

Coverage begins on the date that coverage would otherwise have been lost by reason of a qualifying event and can end when:

- The last day of maximum coverage is reached;
- Premiums are not paid on a timely basis;
- The employer ceases to maintain a group health plan;
- A beneficiary is entitled to Medicare benefits; or
- Coverage is obtained with another employer group health plan that does not contain any exclusion or limitation with respect to any pre-existing condition of such beneficiary.

Although COBRA specifies certain maximum required periods of time that continued health coverage must be offered to qualified beneficiaries, it does not prohibit plans from offering continuation health coverage that goes beyond the COBRA periods.

■ COVERED BENEFITS

Identical Coverage Benefit

Qualified beneficiaries (individuals receiving coverage based on COBRA) must be offered benefits identical to those received immediately before qualifying for continuation coverage. The coverage continuation rules apply to any type of employer-provided group health plan, whether insured or self-insured, funded or self-funded.

---

[1] If a qualified beneficiary is determined under Title II or XVI of the Social Security Act to have been disabled within the first 60 days of COBRA coverage, then the qualified beneficiary and all qualified beneficiaries in his or her family may be able to extend COBRA continuation coverage for an additional 11 months. Notice of the determination must be given to the plan administrator within 60 days of the date of determination and before the end of the 18-month COBRA continuation period.

Health care for this purpose includes indemnity, health maintenance organization (HMO), and preferred provider organization (PPO) plans.

Under COBRA, a group health plan is ordinarily defined as a plan that provides medical benefits for the employer's own employees and their dependents through insurance or another mechanism such as a trust, HMO, self-funded pay-as-you-go-basis, reimbursement, or a combination of these. Medical benefits provided under the terms of the plan and available to COBRA beneficiaries may include:

- Inpatient and outpatient hospital care;
- Physician care;
- Surgery and other major medical benefits;
- Prescription drugs; and
- Any other medical benefits, such as dental and vision care.

Life insurance is not covered under COBRA.

Deductibles and Co-Insurance

The COBRA statute also requires that deductibles and co-insurance amounts for qualified beneficiaries not be greater than those for active employees.

Plan Options

If the plan provides options to covered employees, those options must be made available to qualified beneficiaries. An example of an option would be the right of terminating employees to convert their group coverage to individual health insurance without regard to pre-existing conditions and without having to undergo a medical examination or otherwise demonstrate proof of insurability.

Plan Limitations

The coverage provided to qualified beneficiaries must have the same benefit limits and limits on "out-of-pocket" expenses that are made available to covered employees. Moreover, like deductibles, any amounts already credited to the limits prior to a qualifying event are carried forward into the continuation coverage period.

Core and Non-Core Benefits

A qualified beneficiary, during the period he or she was covered while employed, might have been insured under a policy providing both core and non-core benefits.

Core coverage includes all the health benefits available to the insured other than dental and vision benefits, the only types of coverage defined as non-core.

Under law, qualified beneficiaries may limit coverage to just core-benefits notwithstanding that they had both types of coverage while employed. In other words, it stops the insurer or employer from forcing unwanted coverage and a higher premium on the COBRA-qualified beneficiary.

■ NOTICE AND ELECTION PROCEDURES

Notice by the Employer

An initial notice describing COBRA rights must be furnished to qualified beneficiaries (insured employees and their covered spouses and dependents) when the plan becomes subject to the provisions of COBRA or to new employees and their covered spouses and dependents once they join the plan.

When the employer is not the plan administrator, it must provide notice to the outside administrator within 30 days from the date coverage ceases or the date of the following qualifying events:

- Death of the covered employee;
- Termination of the covered employee for reasons other than gross misconduct;
- The covered employee becoming entitled to Medicare; and
- The employer's bankruptcy.

The administrator, in turn, has 14 days to notify qualified beneficiaries of their COBRA rights due to a qualifying event having occurred.

Notice by the Employee

An employee or spouse must notify the plan administrator (or employer if there is no administrator) of the occurrence of any of the following:

- Divorce
- Legal separation
- Cessation of dependent's eligibility (i.e., loss of dependency status)
- Death of the employee

Notice must be given within 60 days of the qualifying event or the date the qualified beneficiary would lose coverage as a result of the event, whichever is later. The group plan is not obligated to offer the qualified beneficiary the opportunity to elect COBRA coverage, if the covered employee or qualified beneficiary fails to make the required notification.

Notice by Disabled Beneficiaries

A disabled beneficiary is entitled to an extra 11 months of continuation coverage in addition to the 18 months provided by law, if the SSA determines that there was disability within the first 60 days of COBRA coverage. To qualify, disabled beneficiaries must notify the plan administrator of their disability within 60 days of their disability determination and before the end of the 18-month COBRA continuation period.

Election

Qualified beneficiaries are given a 60-day period to elect or reject coverage. This period is measured from the later of the coverage loss date or the date the COBRA election notice is provided.

Although each qualified beneficiary may independently elect coverage, a covered employee or the employee's spouse may elect coverage for all other qualified beneficiaries. A parent or legal guardian may also elect on behalf of a minor child. The law further allows a qualified beneficiary to elect coverage after waiving it, if the election is made within the 60-day period.

■ COST OF COVERAGE

Beneficiaries are required to pay the entire premium for coverage. The premium cannot exceed 102 percent of the cost of the plan to similarly situated individuals who have not incurred a qualifying event, including both the portion paid by employees and any portion paid by the employer before the qualifying event, plus 2 percent for administrative costs. When an employee gets extended coverage due to a disability, the premium charged for months 18 through 29 may be increased to 150 percent of the cost of the plan.

Except for the initial payment, federal law states that payment of a premium is considered timely if made within 30 days after the due date, unless a longer due date is permitted in the plan. Federal law also provides that COBRA coverage can be canceled if premium payments are not made within the 30-day cycle. As to the first payment, a qualified beneficiary has 45 days to pay the premium measured from the date of the COBRA election.

■ CERTIFICATE OF COVERAGE

In order to ensure that a plan or insurer will recognize an individual's prior health coverage, HIPAA requires the issuance of a Certificate of Coverage. This certificate enables an individual to provide evidence of prior creditable coverage in order to reduce or completely avoid any pre-existing condition exclusion that would otherwise limit the coverage of a subsequent group or individual health plan.

Legislation requires that plans and issuers must furnish certificates automatically to:

- An individual entitled to elect COBRA continuation coverage at a time no later than when a notice is required to be provided for a qualifying event under COBRA;
- An individual who loses coverage under a group health plan and who is not entitled to elect COBRA continuation coverage within a reasonable time after coverage ceases; and
- An individual who has elected COBRA continuation coverage either within a reasonable time after a plan learns that COBRA continuation coverage ceased or, if applicable, within a reasonable time after the individual's grace period for the payment of COBRA premiums ends.

A certificate must always be provided at the written request of the participant, the covered spouse, or any of the insured dependents, provided that this request is made within 24 months after the individual loses coverage under the plan. When a certificate is requested, it must disclose each period of continuous coverage.

If the insured has more than 18 months of uninterrupted coverage, the certificate may simply show 18 months of creditable coverage without mentioning dates. If coverage is less than 18 months, the certificate must disclose the dates that coverage commenced and ended. In any case, the certificate needs only to disclose the most recent period of continuous coverage without a 63-day break in coverage.

10

STATE "MINI-COBRA" LAWS

The Consolidated Omnibus Budget Reconciliation Act of 1985 (COBRA) provides for an individual who is working, has group health insurance, and voluntarily resigns from a job or is terminated for any reason other than "gross misconduct" to be given the right to continue the coverage for up to 18 months at his or her expense. This period of coverage is extended to 29 months if the insured is determined to have been disabled within 60 days of becoming eligible for COBRA, and to 36 months for the spouse and dependent children of a covered employee if the employee becomes eligible through the death or divorce of the employee or if the child loses his or her dependent status under the terms of the plan.

In general, three groups of people qualify for COBRA benefits: employees or former employees in private business, their spouses, and their dependent children. Eligibility also extends to workers in state and local government and to workers classified as independent contractors. However, the law exempts an employer with fewer than 20 employees, federal government employers, and certain church-related organizations.

Fortunately, a number of states have taken the initiative of adopting legislation, referred to as "mini-COBRA" laws, which extends many of the benefits of COBRA to state residents who have not qualified under the federal law.

Notwithstanding state legislation, a question is still raised of whether a self-funded plan, not qualifying for COBRA and limited under the federal law ERISA, would be subject to a state's "mini-COBRA" statute. Some states adopt the view that a self-funded plan ERISA preempts a "mini-COBRA" law. Other states take the opposite stand. Because of the conflict, it is suggested that clients participating in self-funded plans not subject to COBRA check with their state's insurance department to find out (a) if the state has a "mini-COBRA" statute and (b) if so, whether coverage could be continued notwithstanding ERISA.

■ "MINI-COBRA" LAWS CURRENTLY IN EFFECT IN 40 STATES

- *Arkansas*—Under state law, continuation of an employee's group coverage includes the following features:
  - An individual insured through an employer-based group health plan has the right to continue his or her coverage for up to 120 days due to termination of employment.
  - Death, divorce, or legal separation of the employee also triggers up to 120 days of continuation coverage for the covered spouse and dependent.
  - The employee must have been insured for a period of at least 3 three months immediately prior to the event triggering the continuation.
- *California*—California has a continuation policy providing limited benefits. The legislation includes the following benefits:
  - An insured in a group health plan has the right to continue his or her health coverage for up to 90 days due to termination of employment.
  - Continuation of 90 days is also extended to dependents who were insured under the previous policy.
  - Coverage ceases when the insured obtains other group insurance even if the terms of the plan are less substantive.
- *Colorado*—Colorado provides a program similar to COBRA for insured groups not subject to that federal law. Some of its features include:
  - Termination of employment of the insured or his or her death, divorce, or legal separation triggers up to 18 months of continuation coverage.
  - The employee must be insured under the employer-based group policy for at least 6 months immediately prior to termination.
  - Continuation is not available to employees and dependents covered under Medicare or Medicaid.
- *Connecticut*—Under state law, continuation of an employer's group health coverage includes the following benefits:
  - The employee, spouse, and dependents have the right to continue their coverage for a period of up to 104 weeks (2 years) if the qualifying event is termination of employment.
  - Connecticut allows up to 156 weeks (3 years) of continuation following the death, divorce, or legal separation of the covered employee.
  - State law requires the employer to send "Notices of Option" within 10 days (and not the 14 or 44 days as permitted under COBRA) to continue the group policy to the covered employee, dependents, and qualified beneficiaries if the loss of coverage is from termination, death, or total disability.

- State law may not be used if COBRA coverage is elected.
- *Florida*—For insured groups not subject to COBRA, Florida has a continuation statute that parallels some of the provisions of the federal law. Some of the features of this legislation include:
  - An individual insured through an employer-based group health plan has the right to continue his or her coverage for up to 18 months if employment is terminated or hours of work reduced.
  - Termination may not be due to the gross misconduct of the employee.
  - Death, divorce, or legal separation of the employee also triggers up to 18 months of continued coverage for insured spouse and dependents.
  - A qualified beneficiary (defined as the covered employee, spouse, and dependent child) is entitled to an additional 11 months of coverage, if he or she becomes disabled as determined by the SSA and notification of the same is provided to the employer within 60 days from the date of determination and prior to the end of the 18-month continuation period.
- *Georgia*—Georgia has a continuation program that provides limited benefits. The legislation includes the following features:
  - An insured has the right to continue his or her health coverage for up to 90 days due to termination of employment.
  - The insured must be covered under the plan for a period of at least 6 months immediately preceding the termination.
  - Following the 90-day extension, the insured has the option to convert the policy to individual coverage.
- *Illinois*—For insured groups not eligible for COBRA, Illinois has a continuation statute providing limited benefits. The legislation includes the following features:
  - A qualifying event includes the termination of the insured's employment (unless termination was due to theft or commission of a work-related felony) as well as the divorce, death, legal separation, or annulment.
  - Continuation of insurance must be offered to employer groups of any size, provided that the insured was covered for three continuous months before a qualifying event.
  - Coverage during continuation must be the same as provided in the group plan, but need not include extra benefits such as prescription drugs.
  - Coverage is a maximum of nine months and premiums may not exceed the group rate.
- *Iowa*—Iowa provides a program similar to COBRA for an individual insured in a group health plan by an employer with 2 to 19 employees. The legislation includes the following benefits:

- The insured must be covered under the policy for a period of at least three months immediately preceding termination of employment.
- Termination of employment or membership in the group policy triggers up to 9 months of continuation coverage.
- The insured's death, divorce, legal separation, or annulment also triggers 9 months of continuation coverage for the covered spouse or legal dependent.
- Coverage ceases if the insured becomes eligible for Medicare or another group plan.

- *Kansas*—Under state law, individuals working in concerns with 2 to 19 employees are entitled to benefits similar to COBRA. The statute includes the following features:
  - An insured in a group has the right to continue his or her health coverage for up to 6 months following termination of employment.
  - The insured's death, divorce, legal separation, or annulment also triggers 6 months of continuation coverage for the covered spouse or legal dependent.
  - The insured must be covered under the group policy at least 3 months immediately preceding a qualifying event.
  - Continuation is not available to someone eligible for Medicare.

- *Kentucky*—Under state law, individuals working in concerns with 2 to 19 employees are entitled to benefits similar to COBRA. The statute includes the following features:
  - The legislation applies to an individual who has been covered under the employer-based group policy for at least 3 months immediately preceding the event triggering the continuation.
  - Continuation of coverage is triggered by the termination of the individual's employment. Divorce, death, or legal separation of the employee also triggers continuation for the spouse and dependent.
  - The extension of insurance is for a period of 18 months.
  - Continuation is not available to an individual who is eligible for Medicare or could be covered under another group plan.

- *Louisiana*—This state has enacted legislation with COBRA-like benefits to individuals working in concerns with 2 to 19 employees. The law includes the following features:
  - An individual who has been insured under a group health policy through his or her employer and has been continuously employed for at least 3 months prior to termination is entitled to up to 12 months of continuation coverage.
  - The insured has 90 days (not just 60 days as provided by COBRA) to exercise this option, and premiums may not exceed the amounts charged under the group plan.

- *Maine*—Under state law, insured groups are entitled to limited benefits. The statute includes the following features:
  - Continuation of coverage for up to 6 months if termination is based on the insured's layoff or a work-related condition.
  - Continuation of coverage may be as long as 12 months, if the employee is totally disabled at the time of election.
- *Maryland*—The state has a statute similar to COBRA, but not as broad. The legislation includes the following benefits:
  - The law provides continuation of coverage for involuntarily laid off employees and their dependents.
  - Continuation coverage will be for a term of up to 18 months, if the insured was covered for at least 30 days before termination.
  - The insurer may charge a premium of up to 102 percent of the group rate.
- *Massachusetts*—Under state law, individuals in insured employer group plans are entitled to continuation similar to COBRA. The legislation includes the following features:
  - Coverage will be up to 39 weeks in the event of layoff.
  - Death of the employee entitles the spouse and dependents to 39 weeks of continuation coverage.
  - The premium on the continuation policy may not exceed the amount charged on the group coverage.
  - Plant closings entitle those individuals insured under the policy to 90 days of continuation coverage.
  - Coverage ceases when the insured becomes eligible for another group plan.
- *Minnesota*—In Minnesota, the statute providing continuation of the employer-based group policy includes the following features:
  - Rules similar to COBRA for small employers (2 to 19 employees) in that the employee has the right to continue health coverage for up to 18 months from the time employment ends.
  - The premium for the new policy may not exceed 102 percent of the group rate.
  - If an insured individual becomes totally disabled while employed, the employer may not terminate or suspend coverage on the grounds that the employee is no longer working. The employee's coverage cannot be terminated as long as the premium is paid, which may be as much as 102 percent of the amount charged for the group plan (the figure of 102 percent, common in many states but greater for some, allows for a 2 percent administration fee).

- Coverage ceases when the insured becomes covered under another group policy.
- *Mississippi*—State continuation policy is limited and includes the following features:
  - An insured in a group health plan has the right to continue his or her health coverage for up to 12 months after termination of employment.
  - The insured must have been covered under the group policy for at least 3 months immediately preceding the qualifying event.
  - Coverage under this provision does not extend to individuals entitled to another group plan, provided that that plan does not contain a provision excluding coverage because of a pre-existing condition.
- *Missouri*—Under state law, continuation of an employee's group coverage includes the following features:
  - A person working for a concern that employs 2 to 19 individuals and is in a fully insured group health plan has the right to continue health coverage for 9 months after his or her job ends.
  - The employee must have been insured for a period of at least 3 months immediately prior to the qualifying event (termination of employment, death, divorce, or legal separation).
  - Coverage will be for a period of 9 months.
- *Nebraska*—Under state law, continuation of an employee's group coverage includes the following features:
  - If the employee is covered under a group health plan and terminated from employment, the insurance will continue for a period of 6 months on a monthly renewal basis.
  - For insured groups not subject to COBRA, death of the employee entitles dependents to up to 1 year of coverage.
  - If coverage is continued, the premium charged may not exceed 102 percent of the group rate.
- *Nevada*—State law provides a program similar to COBRA for an individual insured in a group health plan by an employer with 2 to 19 employees. The legislation includes the following features:
  - If the employee is terminated for any reason other than gross misconduct, coverage will be extended for 18 months.
  - In the case of the termination (other than for gross misconduct), death, divorce, or legal separation of the employee, the extension for a covered spouse or dependent child will be 36 months.
  - These extensions do not apply to an individual who voluntarily resigns.

- The employee, spouse, or dependent child must be insured for a period of at least 12 months immediately preceding the termination of coverage.
- The amount charged for the continuation policy may not exceed 125 percent of the group rate.

- *New Hampshire*—State law also provides a program similar to COBRA. The legislation contains the following features:
  - The legislation applies to an individual who has been employed for at least 6 months. It also extends to the insured's spouse or dependent, if covered under the policy.
  - Continuation of coverage is triggered by the termination of the individual's employment. Divorce and legal separation also trigger continuation.
  - The extension of insurance will be for a period of 18 months, except when the employee becomes disabled at any time during the first 60 days of coverage under this statute. In such case, the term of coverage will be 29 months.
  - The premium may not exceed 102 percent of the amount charged for the group policy.

- *New Jersey*—State law establishes a COBRA-like policy for individuals who had been covered under employer-based group health plans and are no longer working. The features of this legislation include:
  - If an employee who has group coverage is terminated, transferred to part-time status, or ends employment, he or she is given the option of continuing the insurance.
  - The continued coverage will have a term of 12 months.
  - The premium on the new coverage may not exceed 102 percent of the premium paid for similarly situated covered persons.
  - Coverage under state continuation will cease if one of the following occurs:
    - The employer chooses not to provide health benefits to any employees;
    - The employee fails to make payment of the premium in a timely manner;
    - The employee becomes covered under another health plan that contains no limitation or exclusion as to a pre-existing condition, or if there is a pre-existing condition clause in the policy and the period excluding coverage has ended;
    - The person covered under the continuation policy becomes eligible for Medicare; or
    - In the case of dependents who are continuing as part of the employee's continuation election, the person no longer meets the policy's definition of a "dependent."

- *New Mexico*—The state continuation policy is limited and includes the following:
  - If the employee has employer-based group health insurance and the employment is terminated, coverage may be extended for a period of 6 months.
  - Death, divorce, or legal separation also triggers up to 6 months of continuation coverage for the insured spouse and dependent.
- *New York*—The New York law authorizing continuation of a group health policy closely parallels the federal COBRA statute. The statute includes the following features:
  - In case of the termination of the employee, group health coverage insuring this individual and his or her dependents may be extended for a period of 18 months.
  - Election to continue must be exercised by the employee within 60 days following the termination or the date he or she was sent notification of continuation by the group policyholder, whichever is later.
  - Continuation does not apply to an employee who is eligible for another group policy, provided that it does not contain a pre-existing condition limitation.
  - Continuation does not apply to an employee eligible for Medicare.
  - If the employee is determined to have been disabled under SSDI standards at any time during the first 60 days of continuation of coverage, the coverage may be extended to a period of 29 months.
- *North Carolina*—The North Carolina law provides a COBRA-like policy for employees experiencing termination of employment. The legislation includes the following features:
  - If an employee is insured through an employer-sponsored health policy and is terminated from work, he or she will be able to continue coverage for himself, and for eligible spouses and other dependents, for a period of 18 months.
  - The premium for the continuation policy is not to be more than the group rate.
- *North Dakota*—Under state law, continuation of an employee's group coverage includes the following features:
  - The employee must have been insured for a period of at least 3 continuous months ending with the termination.
  - Continuation is not available to those employees or dependents who are covered under Medicare.
  - If an employee is insured through an employer-sponsored health policy and is terminated from work, he or she will be able to continue coverage for himself and an eligible spouse and other dependents for a term of up to 39 months.

- When continuation is due to the termination of employment, the premium charged on a continuation policy may not be more than that charged for the group coverage. However, when triggered by divorce, the premium may be as high as 102 percent of the group rate.

- *Ohio*—State law provides a program that continues health coverage for an individual insured in a group health plan sponsored by an employer regardless of whether it is subject to COBRA. The legislation includes the following features:
  - The employee must be covered under the group policy for a period of 3 months immediately preceding the termination of his or her employment.
  - Continuation does not extend to individuals who are covered under Medicare.
  - The term of the continuation policy is 6 months.
  - Spouses and dependents of reservists called to active duty may extend coverage up to 36 months if the reservist dies.

- *Oklahoma*—The state continuation policy is limited. It covers the following:
  - If an individual has group health coverage through his or her employer and the insurance is terminated, the employee and dependents will remain insured for a period of at least 30 days following the termination.

- *Oregon*—Oregon's continuation policy legislation covers the following features:
  - If an individual (certificate holder) has group health coverage through his or her employer and the employment has terminated, the employee and dependents may remain insured for a period of 6 months.
  - The extension commences on the date of termination.
  - Coverage will cease if the certificate holder becomes eligible for Medicare.

- *Rhode Island*—Under state law, the plan will continue for a period of 18 months if the employer provides group health insurance to an employee whose coverage is then terminated because of involuntary layoff, death, the workplace ceasing to exist, or the permanent reduction in size of the workforce. Other features of the statute include:
  - The extension covers both the employee and eligible dependents and spouse.
  - The cost of insurance may not exceed the premium charged for the group coverage.

- *South Carolina*—South Carolina's continuation policy legislation includes the following:
  - If an individual has group health coverage through employment and the policy is terminated for any reason other than non-payment of the premium, the insured is entitled to continue coverage for 6 months plus any fraction of the month remaining.

- The employee must be insured under the policy for at least 6 months immediately preceding termination.
- The employer is required to inform the employee of the right to continue coverage following termination of the policy. Notification will be at the time of termination.
- The premium charged for the extended coverage may not exceed the group rate.
- *South Dakota*—The state has legislation similar to COBRA and includes the following features:
  - The statute applies only to companies with fewer than 20 employees.
  - Coverage will continue for a term of 18 months.
  - Continuation is only available to the employee who had coverage under the group policy during the entire 6-month period prior to the termination.
- *Tennessee*—Under state law, continuation of an employee's group policy coverage includes the following features:
  - For insured groups not subject to COBRA, death, divorce, or legal separation triggers up to 15 months of continuation coverage, but premiums must be paid in 3-month increments.
  - Termination of employment triggers up to three months of continuation coverage if the individual was insured continuously for at least 3 months immediately preceding termination.
- *Texas*—Under state law, continuation of the group health coverage includes the following features:
  - An employee's termination of insurance triggers up to 6 months of continuation coverage, provided that the employee had been covered for at least 3 months immediately preceding termination.
  - Death, divorce, or legal separation triggers up to 3 years' continuation coverage for the employee's spouse and dependent, provided that they were covered continuously for at least 1 year before the qualifying event.
  - The premium for continuation coverage may not exceed 102 percent of the group rate.
- *Utah*—The state continuation policy is limited. It includes the following features:
  - An employee's termination of group insurance triggers up to 6 months of continuous coverage, provided that the insured group is not subject to COBRA and the termination is not due to gross misconduct.
  - The new coverage will terminate prior to the completion of the 6-month term if one of the following occurs:
    - The terminated insured establishes residency outside the state of Utah;
    - Failure to make timely payment of the premium;

- Violation of a material condition of the policy or the employer's coverage is terminated; or
- The employer replaces the insurance with a similar group policy coverage.

■ *Vermont*—The state has a statute similar to COBRA, but it is not as broad. The legislation includes the following benefits and limitations:
  - An individual who has been insured under an employer-based group health policy and has been continuously covered for a period of 3 months immediately preceding termination is entitled to up to 6 months of coverage.
  - The right of continuation does not extend to individuals eligible for another group plan or Medicare.
  - For insured groups not subject to COBRA, death of an employee triggers up to 6 months of continuation coverage for spouses and dependents.

■ *Virginia*—Virginia has a limited COBRA-like statute. The legislation includes the following benefits and limitations:
  - For insured groups not subject to COBRA, termination of employment triggers up to 90 days of continuation coverage, provided that insured was covered continuously for at least 3 months immediately preceding termination.
  - Continuation does not apply to individuals who are eligible for other group coverage or Medicare.
  - The premium for a continuation policy may not exceed the group rate.

■ *Washington*—For insured groups, Washington has a continuation statute that includes the following features:
  - The law is not based on coverage through employment. Instead, it requires insurers that provide group health coverage to offer the policyholder the option to include continuation coverage for any person becoming ineligible for any reason.
  - The premium charged is one agreed to by the policyholder and insurer.
  - The option provided by law requires the policyholder and insurer to negotiate the terms triggering continuation of coverage.

■ *West Virginia*—For insured groups not subject to COBRA, West Virginia has a continuation statute that includes the following features:
  - Coverage will be up to 18 months when an employee who is insured under an employer-sponsored group policy is involuntarily terminated.
  - The continuation applies to all individuals insured by such group coverage.

■ *Wisconsin*—For insured groups not subject to COBRA, Wisconsin has a continuation statute that either parallels or is more liberal than the federal statute. The more important features include:
  - Continuation extends for a term of 18 months when an employee who is insured under an employer-sponsored group policy is terminated.

- Notice of option to continue coverage must be sent within 5 days (not the 44 days permitted by COBRA) to the insured employee, dependents, or qualified beneficiaries, if the loss of coverage is due to termination of employment, death, or total disability.
- The premium may not exceed the group rate.
- Continuation coverage ceases if one of the following occurs:
  - The terminated insured establishes residency outside the state of Wisconsin;
  - The terminated insured fails to make timely payment of the premium; or
  - The terminated insured becomes eligible for similar coverage.

■ *Wyoming*—For insured groups not subject to the federal statute of COBRA, the state of Wisconsin offers the following:
- The continuation of COBRA for a fully insured group health plan, or a state or local government plan, with 2 to 19 employees.
- Coverage of up to 12 months when the employee's job ends.

11

TICKET TO WORK AND WORK INCENTIVES IMPROVEMENT ACT OF 1999

■ OVERVIEW OF LEGISLATION

On December 17, 1999, President Clinton signed into law the Ticket to Work and Work Incentives Improvement Act of 1999 (TWWIIA). TWWIIA was enacted to make it easier for individuals with disabilities to retain their Medicare benefits longer when returning to work and to remove limits on the Medicaid buy-in options for workers with disabilities. The Act also expands options for rehabilitation and vocational services. It is being phased in over a four-year period beginning in 2000.

In his comments at the time of passage, Mr. Clinton noted that it was the fear of losing health insurance that kept people with disabilities from seeking employment. This dilemma placed people with disabilities receiving Social Security and wanting to work in a "double bind," since keeping health benefits required staying out of the workforce and on Social Security. This paradox "defies common sense and economic logic. This is about more than jobs and paychecks. It is fundamentally about the dignity of each human being… [in] recognizing that work is at the heart of the American dream." Fear of losing insurance should not keep people from seeking employment.

■ THE TWWIIA ACT

TWWIIA extends to 8-1/2 years the premium-free Medicare Part A benefits for people on SSD who return to work. This means limiting the monthly premium to $54 for Medicare Part B coverage nationwide. The legislation also bars the SSA from medically reviewing a beneficiary solely because of his or her work activity.

In addition, the Act requires that, if the insured is disabled, entitled to Medicare Part A benefits, and becomes covered under a group health plan through employment (provided that the employer has 20 or more employees), the premiums for any Medigap plan covering the insured may be suspended at his or her request. If the insured loses the employer coverage after receiving such group insurance and suspending Medigap premiums and benefits, the Medigap policy must restore benefits. (However, the renewal of coverage becomes effective only if the individual provides notice of the loss within 90 days of such event.)

■ INCENTIVES TO STATES

The TWWIIA allows states to make the following changes to Medicaid:

- Make Medicaid available to individuals between the ages of 16 and 64 who because of income earned from work, are ineligible to receive Supplemental Security Income (SSI) and
- Extend Medicaid to employed persons with disabilities whose medical condition has improved, but who have continued to have a "severe medically determinable impairment" as defined by the federal Health and Human Services Regulations.

The decision to make these changes to Medicaid is determined by each state. The status of a state's legislation pursuant to this Act can be provided by its Department of Insurance.

Persons in states exercising these options, who previously would not have qualified for Medicaid, now:

- Are permitted to buy into Medicaid coverage by paying premiums and other cost-sharing charges on a sliding fee-scale based on income.
- May be required by the state to pay the full premium if their incomes exceed 250 percent of the federal poverty level.
- Are guaranteed that premiums may not exceed 7.5 percent of income if their incomes are between 250 and 450 percent of the federal poverty level.

For individuals with annual adjusted gross incomes (as defined by the Internal Revenue Service) exceeding $75,000, states are required to charge 100 percent of the premiums imposed. However, the statute does permit states to subsidize the premium cost for individuals using state funds.

12

COMPREHENSIVE STATE HEALTH INSURANCE FOR HIGH-RISK INDIVIDUALS[1]

High-risk pools have been created by 29 states to provide an insurance option to those who are considered medically uninsurable or high risk. These programs offer an insurance alternative to individuals who have been denied health insurance coverage due to a serious health condition, or whose insurance premiums have escalated beyond those charged in the high-risk pool.

Eligibility for these programs varies from state to state. For several states, individuals are qualified if they meet the standards of federal eligibility.

Federal eligibility criteria are as follows:

- Current residents of the state.
- Have had continuous creditable coverage of 18 months or more, at least the last day of which was under a group health plan or government plan.
- Are not eligible for coverage under a group health plan, Medicare, or Medicaid.
- Have not had a break in coverage of 63 or more days from the time the previous insurance was terminated.
- Must have exhausted any COBRA or state program with similar benefits.

The states that base eligibility on these federal criteria are noted in the summaries below.

---

[1] The information in this chapter was collected from several sources including:
- The manual entitled Comprehensive Health Insurance for High-Risk Individuals—A State-by-State Analysis, Communicating for Agriculture, 1999 and
- State offices for high-risk insurance pools
- Georgetown University Web site entitled www.healthinsuranceinfo.net

■ ALABAMA

Organization Administering Insurance and Contact:

A. Organization—Alabama Health Insurance

B. State contact—Alabama Health Insurance Plan (AHIP)
c/o State Employees Insurance Board
P.O. Box 304900
Montgomery, AL 36130-4900
877-619-2447

Eligibility Criteria and Premium Cap:

The applicant:

- Must be an Alabama resident;
- Must be eligible for portability under the Health Insurance and Portability and Accountability Act (HIPAA);
- Must have had at least 18 months of continuous previous coverage;
- Must have exhausted COBRA coverage if eligible;
- Must have not had a break in coverage of 63 or more days from the time the previous insurance was terminated;
- Must have been last insured under either a group health plan, a government plan, or a church plan; and
- Must not have had previous coverage terminated because of fraud or failure to pay premiums.

Premium cap—The cap is fixed at 200 percent of the standard market rate for comparable health insurance.

Waiting Period for Pre-Existing Conditions and Waiver of Waiting Period

- *Waiting period for pre-existing conditions*—None
- *Waiver of waiting period*—None

Coverage:

Two companies provide high-risk insurance in Alabama—Blue Cross and Blue Shield and United Health Care.

Blue Cross administers a traditional indemnity plan that offers annual deductibles of $1,000 and $2,500. The plan with the $1,000 deductible (Plan C) has an inpatient hospital deductible of $500 per stay. The plan with the $2,500 deductible (Plan D) has an inpatient hospital deductible of $500 per stay with an added $100 deductible per day for the 2nd through 11th days.

Both the C and D plans limit the annual out-of-pocket costs to $1,500 per person plus any hospital stay deductible amount. Once the deductible amounts are reached, both plans pay 80 percent of the usual, reasonable, and customary charges of the item covered. After the out-of-pocket limit is reached, the plans pay 100 percent of that charge.

United Health Care makes available an HMO plan with no deductible except for prescription drugs. Features of this plan include:

- Inpatient hospital expense—$500 co-pay
- Outpatient care/doctor visits—$20 co-pay
- Prescription drug coverage (with a maximum annual benefit, per insured, of $1,500)—$50 deductible, $15 co-pay generic, $20 co-pay brand
- Ambulance—$100 co-pay
- Skilled nursing care—limited to 30 days
- Home health visits—limited to 60 visits per year
- Durable medical equipment—no co-pay—limited to $1,500 per year
- Physical therapy—$20 co-pay—limited to 20 visits per year

ALASKA

Organization Administering Insurance and Contact:

A. Organization—Alaska Comprehensive Health Insurance (ACHI)

B. State contact—Alaska Division of Insurance
550 W. 7th Street
15th Floor
Anchorage, AK 99503
800-467-8725
907-269-7900

Eligibility Criteria and Premium Cap:

A. Under the State High-Risk Rules, a person is eligible for coverage if:

- Applicant has been a resident of the state for a period of at least 12 months;
- Applicant is not eligible to have been covered under the state's small employer health insurance plan (2 to 50 employees);

- Applicant is not insured under another health plan, including a government health plan (i.e., Medicare) or a group health plan; and
- At least one of the following has occurred:
  1. Applicant has received notice of rejection for health insurance from at least one health insurer;
  2. Applicant has one of the listed conditions qualifying the applicant for coverage; or
  3. Applicant has received restrictive riders that substantially reduce coverage.

B. Under the federal rules, a person is also eligible for coverage if:

- Domiciled in the State of Alaska;
- Has had 18 months of prior health coverage without a break of 90-days in coverage;
- The person's most recent health insurance was structured as a group plan;
- The person's most recent coverage was not terminated because of fraud or non-payment of a premium;
- The person is not eligible for Medicare, Medicaid, Indian Health Services, or other group health insurance coverage; and
- The person is not covered under another health insurance plan.

Premium cap—The cap is fixed at 200 percent of the standard rate for comparable coverage.

Waiting Period for Pre-Existing Conditions and Waiver of Waiting Period:
- *Waiting period*—If the individual is not federally eligible, coverage will not be extended to expenses incurred during the first six months following the effective date of coverage for any condition if (a) the condition manifested itself within the three-month period immediately preceding the effective date of coverage, or (b) medical advice, care, or treatment was recommended or received as to such condition within the first three-month period immediately preceding the effective date of coverage.
- *Waiver of waiting period*—If the insured's previous plan was involuntarily terminated, the time covered under the earlier policy will be credited toward the pre-existing condition period of the new state policy, provided that the person applies for the new plan within 31 days after termination of the previous contract.

Coverage:

The policies offered include:

A. A major medical PPO plan with per-individual deductibles at $1,000, $1,500, $2,500, $5,000, and $10,000. For the $1,000 deductible, the insured is subject to a $2,500 out-of-pocket expense limitation; for the $1,500 deductible, a $3,000 out-of-pocket limit; for the $2,500 deductible, a $5,000 out-of-pocket limit; for the $5,000 deductible, a $10,000 out-of-pocket limit; and for the $10,000 deductible, a $15,000 out-of-pocket limit. The annual deductible is the amount that the insured must pay each calendar year for eligible expenses before the plan pays benefits, and the out-of-pocket expense limitation is the maximum amount to be paid any calendar year. Once the deductible is paid, the insurer is responsible for 80 percent of the usual and customary charge for in-network expenses and 60 percent of such charge for out-of-network costs. Once the out-of-pocket amounts are paid, the insurance picks up 100 percent of the provider charges regardless of whether it is in-network or out-of-network.

B. A major medical indemnity plan with a single deductible of $1,000 and an out-of-pocket limitation of $2,500.

C. A Medicare carveout plan, which is the same as the indemnity plan, except for lower premiums for the insured and the coordination of benefits between ACHI and Medicare.

The benefits offered under the Alaska plan include the following:

- Inpatient hospital expense
- Outpatient care/doctor visits
- Prescription drug coverage
- Ambulance
- Skilled nursing care—120 days per year
- Home health care—maximum of 270 visits per year
- Durable medical equipment
- Physical therapy

■ ARKANSAS

Organization Administering Insurance and Contact:

A. Organization—The Arkansas Comprehensive Health Insurance Plan (CHIP)

B. State contact—Life and Health Division/Arkansas Insurance Department
1200 West Third Street
Little Rock, AR 72201-1904
501-371-2766
800-224-6330

Eligibility Criteria and Premium Cap:

Individuals qualify if they are federally eligible.

An individual who is not federally eligible will also qualify if he or she meets the following criteria:

- Is a resident of Arkansas for a period of at least 30 days; and
- Was rejected by an insurer for substantially similar coverage because of a pre-existing medical condition; or
- Was offered coverage in excess of the premium for high-risk insurance; or
- Has one of the listed conditions qualifying the applicant for coverage; and
- Is not eligible for or already has similar coverage from another health plan.

Premium cap—The premium is capped at 150 percent of the standard rate for comparable coverage.

Waiting Period for Pre-Existing Conditions and Waiver of Waiting Period:

- *Waiting period*—If the individual is not federally eligible, coverage will not be extended to expenses incurred during the first six months following the effective date of coverage for any condition if (a) the condition manifested itself within the six-month period immediately preceding the effective date of coverage, or (b) medical advice, care, or treatment was recommended or received as to such condition within the first six-month period immediately preceding the effective date of coverage.
- *Waiver of waiting period*—The applicant is either federally eligible or his or her previous plan was involuntarily terminated. The time covered under the earlier policy will be credited toward the pre-existing condition period of the new state policy provided that the person applies for the new plan within 31 days after termination of the previous contract.

Coverage:

The Arkansas plan is structured as a PPO with three deductible amounts offered—$1,000, $5,000, and $10,000. Once the deductible selected is met, there will be an 80/20 payment made for in-network expenses and a 60/40 payment for out-of-network expenses until the covered expenses reach $5,000 for a $1,000 deductible; $25,000 for a $5,000 deductible; or $50,000 for a $10,000 deductible. All covered expenses incurred thereafter during the plan year are paid at 100 percent.

The benefits offered in the Arkansas plan include the following:

- Hospital services
- Professional services for the diagnosis or treatment of injuries or conditions other than dental, which are rendered by a physician or by others at his or her direction
- Drugs requiring a physician's prescription
- Services of a licensed skilled nursing facility for individuals ineligible for Medicare, for not more than 180 calendar days during a policy year, provided that the services are of the type that would qualify as reimbursable services under Medicare
- Services of a home health agency
- Rental or purchase, as appropriate, of durable medical equipment
- Services of a physical therapist and diagnostic X-rays and laboratory tests

■ CALIFORNIA

Organization Administering Insurance and Contact:

A. Organization—California Major Medical Insurance

B. State contact—Managed Risk Medical Insurance Program (MRMIP)
   P.O. Box 2769
   Sacramento, CA 95812-2769
   916-324-4695

Eligibility Criteria and Premium Cap:

In order to be eligible for coverage, the insured must meet the following criteria:

- Be a resident of the State of California;
- Not be eligible for Part A and Part B of Medicare; and
- Not be eligible for COBRA or Cal-COBRA benefits.

- Be able to demonstrate an inability to secure adequate coverage within the previous 12 months due to being:
  - Denied insurance coverage;
  - Involuntarily terminated for reasons other than non-payment of premium or fraud;
  - Requested to pay premium in excess of the program subscriber rate; or
  - A member of a group of one who has been denied coverage.

Premium cap—The cap is fixed at 125 percent of the standard market rate for comparable health insurance unless a plan exceeding the average cost to the state is selected, in which case the premium will be 137.5 percent of the standard rate.

Waiting Period for Pre-Existing Conditions, Waiver of Waiting Period, and Wait List for Program:

- *Waiting period for pre-existing conditions*—For individuals enrolling in the pool's PPO plan, coverage is excluded during a 90-day period following the effective date of coverage for any condition for which medical advice, care, or treatment was recommended or received during the six months immediately preceding enrollment.

  For individuals enrolling in the pool's HMO plan, there is a post-enrollment waiting period of 90 days. Subscribers will not be eligible for benefits during this period.

- *Waiver of waiting period*—The waiting period may be waived in part or all if the subscriber:
  - Has been on the pool's waiting list for a period of at least six months;
  - Has been insured under another health policy for at least 90 days at the time application for MRMIP was made, or was insured under another plan and eligibility for MRMIP was made within 30 days following the termination of that coverage; or
  - Was insured under a high-risk plan offered in another state within the previous 12 months.

- *Waitlist*—The California program maintains a waiting list for new enrollees. The average wait is four to six months, which is credited toward the waiting period.

Coverage:

Five insurance plans are offered by the Major Risk Medical Insurance Program. The following is a brief description of each plan:

A. *Blue Cross of California*—The plan is structured as a PPO with no annual deductible. There is prescription drug coverage consisting of pharmacy and mail order service, a limitation in the co-pay for office visits to in-network doctors of $25, and an out-of-pocket maximum for in-network services of $2,500 per insured with a $4,000 maximum per family.

B. *Access + HMO*—The plan provides each subscriber with a personal physician who coordinates all health care needs, including medically necessary X-ray, laboratory, emergency, and hospital services. The charge for physician care within the group is $15 co-pay for office visits, and the cost of prescriptive drugs is fixed at $10 for generic and $15 for brand name medications. The maximum annual amount in co-payments is $2,500 per individual and $4,000 per family.

C. *Blue Shield Preferred Plan*—In this plan, a subscriber may choose any physician or hospital he or she wants. The cost for an in-network physician varies depending on the deductible selected by the insured. Deductibles range from $500 to $2,500. Details on the various policies can be obtained by calling 800-431-2309.

D. *Kaiser Permanente Northern California Region*—The insurer arranges medical care at its medical facilities. Laboratories, X-ray services, and pharmacies are also located in the facilities. The plan has no deductible and the out-of-pocket maximum is $2,500 per covered person and $4,000 per family. Physician care is $15 co-pay per office visit and prescription drugs are $10 for generic and $25 for brand names, for up to a 100-day supply.

E. *Kaiser Permanente Southern California*—The benefits are the same as the Kaiser Permanente Northern California plan.

■ COLORADO

Organization Administering Insurance and Contact:
A. Organization—Colorado Uninsurable Health Insurance Plan (CUHIP)
B. State contact—CUHIP
   425 S. Cherry Street
   Suite 160
   Denver, CO 80203
   303-863-1960

Eligibility Criteria and Premium Cap:
- Applicant must be a U.S. citizen or have legal alien status.
- Applicant must be a permanent resident of Colorado for at least six months, not delinquent in the payment of Colorado income taxes, and meet one of the following conditions after having applied for health coverage:
  – The application was rejected because of a medical condition;

- The application was accepted, but the premium was higher than the premium under the state's high-risk plan;
- The application was accepted, but treatment of pre-existing health conditions would be permanently excluded; or
- The applicant has one of the medical conditions listed in the insurance application form.

Premium cap—The premium is capped at 150 percent of the standard rate for comparable coverage.

Waiting Period for Pre-Existing Conditions and Waiver of Waiting Period:

- *Waiting period for pre-existing conditions*—Coverage is excluded during the six-month period following the effective date of coverage for any condition that was recommended or received during the six-month period immediately preceding enrollment medical advice, care, or treatment.
- *Waiver of waiting period*—Full or partial waiver of waiting period is offered to those individuals who had qualifying previous coverage that had been terminated no more than 90 days prior to the CUHIP coverage.

Coverage:

Colorado offers only a PPO. The plan includes the following features:

- Deductible—The deductible amounts offered for the PPO are $300, $500, $750, and $2,000
- Outpatient care/doctor visits—PPO for an in-network provider is 80/20. The cost for an out-of-network provider will be 50 percent
- Inpatient hospital expense—PPO has the same co-insurance as provided for doctor visits
- Prescription drug coverage—50 percent co-payment up to a maximum of $30. Insured must use Prescription Network Pharmacy to receive benefit
- Ambulance
- Home health care—60 visits per year
- Physical therapy—PPO pre-certification required for more than six visits
- Annual participant out-of-pocket maximum—Out-of-pocket maximum will vary according to plan deductible that is selected.

CONNECTICUT

Organization Administering Insurance and Contact:

A. Organization—Connecticut Health Reinsurance Association (CHRA)

B. State contact—United Healthcare
450 Columbus Blvd., 9NB
P.O. Box 150450
Hartford, CT 06115-0450
800-842-0004

Eligibility Criteria and Premium Cap:

The individual applying for coverage must be a state resident between the ages of 19 and 65. Unlike a number of state plans, Connecticut does require the applicant to be rejected by a health insurer prior to applying for its plan. In addition, Connecticut offers a low-income plan wherein the insured pays only 75 percent of the Medicare reimbursement level (established for medical services) after the calendar year deductible is paid. For an individual, the deductible is $200 and for a family, it is $400.

Individuals also qualify if they are federally eligible.

Premium cap—The initial premium may not be greater than 125 percent of the standard charge for comparable coverage. For future premiums, the cap is increased to 150 percent.

Waiting Period for Pre-Existing Conditions and Waiver of Waiting Period:

- *Individual policy*—If the insured was covered under an individual policy and has an existing medical condition, coverage is excluded for the first 12 months following the effective date of the CHRA policy. Coverage is also excluded during this 12-month period for the individual policyholder as to any condition for which treatment was received during the 6-month period immediately preceding enrollment.
- *Group insurance*—If the insured was covered under a qualifying group plan:
  - For more than 12 months, there is no pre-existing coverage limitations.
  - For less than 12 months, coverage for a pre-existing condition will be provided under the CHRA policy when the insured has been covered for a total of 12 months between the prior group policy and the CHRA policy.
- *Federal eligibility*—The waiting period is waived if the insured is federally eligible.

Coverage:

The Connecticut program offers two plans, one with HMO coverage and the other structured as a PPO. The Administrator for both plans is United Health Care.

The HMO plan has a maximum out-of-pocket cost per individual for in-network providers of $2,500 and per family of $5,000. There is no annual deductible (except for hospital and skilled nursing services), a $10 co-payment for physician visit, a $10 co-payment for home health care, and a $5 co-payment for each outpatient prescription drug.

The deductible for inpatient hospitalization and skilled nursing at a facility is $500 per admission. Hospitalization as an outpatient is $10 co-payment per visit except for the emergency room, which requires a $25 co-payment.

The PPO plan also has a $2,500 per individual maximum out-of-pocket cost when the insured uses an in-network provider. The family out-of-pocket maximum is $5,000. Some of the other fixed charges in the PPO include:

	In-Network	Out-of-Network
Annual Deductible	$500 per calendar year per individual $1,000 per calendar year per family	$1,000 per calendar year per individual $2,000 per calendar year per family
Physician Services		
Office Visits	80% after deductible	60% after deductible
Inpatient surgery	80% after deductible	60 percent after deductible
Outpatient surgery	80% after deductible	60 percent after deductible
Hospital Services		
Inpatient	80% after deductible	60% after deductible
Outpatient	80% after deductible	60% after deductible
Emergency Room	80% after deductible	60% after deductible
X-Ray & Lab Exams	80% after deductible	60% after deductible
Outpatient Drugs	80% after deductible	60% after deductible

■ FLORIDA

Organization Administering Insurance and Contact:

A. Organization—The Florida Comprehensive Health Association (FCHA)

B. State contact—FCHA
1210 E. Park Avenue
Tallahassee, FL 32301
850-309-1200

NOTE: The Florida Legislature closed new enrollment in the plan effective June 30, 1991.

Eligibility Criteria and Premium Cap:

Participants must be a resident of the State of Florida and have received from two or more health insurers:

- Notice of rejection for substantially similar insurance;
- Notice of benefit reduction for specific condition exclusion; or
- Notice of premium increase for in-force or applied-for insurance exceeding the rate established for the high-risk insurance.

Premium cap—For a high-risk individual, it is 250 percent of the standard rate for comparable coverage. Someone diagnosed with MS or a similar long-term condition is considered a high-risk individual.

Waiting Period for Pre-Existing Condition and Waiver of Waiting Period:

- *Waiting period*—Coverage is excluded during the 12-month period following the effective date of coverage for any condition for which care or treatment was recommended or received during the 6-month period immediately preceding enrollment medical advice.
- *Waiver of waiting period*—None

Coverage:

FCHA offers a $1,000, $1,500, $2,000, $5,000, and $10,000 deductible.

FCHA has structured its policy to ensure that the participant will be covered under one of three services: the case management service, or preferred provider network service, and standard service.

The case management service is for individuals who are considered high-risk insured. The service becomes effective once it is determined by a team of medical managers that such a program will be more cost-effective and provide better quality care to the individual insured.

FCHA also has a preferred provider network service, which will pay 80 percent of covered costs for the first $10,000 and 90 percent of covered costs thereafter. The third service pays 60 percent of covered costs for the first $10,000, after which it will pay 70 percent of covered costs.

Coverage provided in the Florida plan, regardless of the service utilized, includes: outpatient doctor visits, inpatient hospital care, home health visits (120 day limit), necessary durable medical equipment, physical therapy (21-day limit per 6 months), and prescription drug coverage.

ILLINOIS

Organization Administering Insurance and Contact:

A. Organization—Illinois Comprehensive Health Insurance (ICHI)

B. State contact—ICHIP
400 W. Monroe Street, Suite 202
Springfield, IL 62704
217-558-6202

Eligibility Criteria and Premium Cap:

Federal eligibility applies in Illinois.
Three types of plans are offered in the Illinois high-risk pool:

- Plan 2 is only available to individuals who are enrolled in Parts A and B of Medicare due to a disability or have end-stage renal disease.
- Plan 3 is a PPO plan available to individuals who are not federally eligible and are therefore subject to up to a six-month waiting period for a pre-existing condition.
- Plan 5 is also a PPO plan for individuals who are federally eligible. There is no pre-existing condition limitation and inpatient treatment of mental illness is limited to 45 days per calendar year for all hospitals.

Federal eligibility allows individuals to avoid a pre-existing condition waiting period, even if they have changed insurance plans.

Those individuals who are not federally eligible and are applying for Plans 2 or 3 must:

- Be a U.S. citizen or permanent resident alien;
- Be a resident of Illinois for at least 180 days;
- Have applied to an insurance company within the last 9 months and received a rejection or refusal to issue the insurance for health reasons by one insurer; or
- Have received a refusal to issue or renew substantially similar individual health coverage at a rate exceeding the amount charged for the ICHIP plan; or
- Have been diagnosed with one of 31 presumptive medical conditions.

Since the inception of the program in May of 1989, there have only been three increases in the premium rates charged, and rates have remained stable since 1994. The premium is based on the insured's age, sex, and the county of residence.

Waiver Period for Pre-Existing Condition and Waiver of Waiting Period:

- *Waiting period*—For those individuals who are not federally eligible, coverage is excluded during the six-month period following the effective date of coverage for any condition for which medical advice, care, or treatment was recommended or received during the six-month period immediately preceding the enrollment.

- *Waiver of waiting period*—A waiver is granted if the insurance immediately preceding the ICHI policy was involuntarily terminated; if the individual is ineligible for any continuation or conversion rights; if application for ICHI and waiver is made within 90 days following termination; and with payment of an additional 10 percent increase in the regular premium for the life of the policy or 60 months, whichever is less.

Coverage:

Illinois offers three plans, two of which are structured as PPOs and one as a major medical plan. The annual individual deductibles and out-of-pocket expense limits for these plans are as follows:

Plan	Deductible	Out-of-pocket limits
Plan 2	$500	$2,000
Plan 2	$1,000	$2,500
Plan 2	$1,500	$3,000
Plan 2	$2,500	$4,000
Plans 3 & 5	$500	$2,000 + $4,500 Non-PPO Expenses
Plans 3 & 5	$1,000	$2,500 + $4,500 Non-PPO Expenses
Plans 3 & 5	$1,500	$3,000 + $4,500 Non-PPO Expenses
Plans 3 & 5	$2,500	$4,000 + $4,500 Non-PPO Expenses

The annual lifetime maximum amount, regardless of the plan, is $1,000,000. The benefits provided under the Illinois plans include:

- Daily room and board and other hospital services
- Drugs and medicines requiring a written prescription
- Purchase or rental of durable medical equipment
- Skilled nursing care benefits limited to 120 days in a skilled nursing facility each calendar year
- Physical therapy
- Outpatient care and doctor visits

■ INDIANA

Organization Administering Insurance and Contact:

A. Organization—Indiana Comprehensive Health Insurance Association (ICHIA)

B. State contact—ICHIA
Outsourced Administrative Systems, Inc.
4550 Victory Lane
Indianapolis, IN 46203
800-552-7921 (Indiana Only)
317-614-2133

Eligibility Criteria and Premium Cap:

- Participants must be a resident of the state for at least 90 days immediately preceding the application for insurance;
- They may not be enrolled in Medicaid;
- They may not be eligible for a group health insurance plan, and they must receive or qualify for one of the following:
    - A notice of rejection for substantially similar insurance;
    - A notice of benefit reduction below the minimum requirements of health insurance in the state;
    - A notice of premium increase for similar coverage that exceeds the pool rate; or
    - A diagnosis with a medical condition that automatically qualifies the applicant for ICHIA.

An individual will also qualify if he or she is federally eligible.

Premium cap—The figure is capped at 150 percent of the standard rate for comparable coverage.

Waiting Period with Pre-Existing Condition and Waiver of Waiting Period:

- *Waiting period*—Coverage is excluded during the three-month period following the effective date of coverage for any condition for which medical advice, care, or treatment was recommended or received during the three-month period immediately preceding enrollment.
- *Waiver of waiting period*—The waiting period is waived if the participant was covered for health insurance and lost coverage within six months prior to application for ICHIA insurance. Federal eligibility also allows individuals to avoid a pre-existing condition waiting period.

Coverage:

Three PPO plans are offered. After the deductible is met, reasonable and customary expenses for in-network charges are covered at an 80/20 ratio. Out-of-network charges are covered at a 60/40 ratio.

Plan 1 has a $500 deductible with no limitation on the maximum benefit that may be paid. The out-of-pocket limit for an individual is $1,000 and for a family, $2,500.

Plan 2 has a $1,000 deductible with a limitation of $100,000 for a transplant and $50,000 for a mental or nervous disorder. The out-of-pocket limit for an individual is $2,000 and for a family, $2,500.

Plan 3 has a $1,500 deductible with a limitation of $100,000 for a transplant and $50,000 for a mental or nervous disorder. The out-of-pocket limit for an individual is $2,500 and for a family, $5,000.

The following is covered under the three plans:

- Inpatient hospital care up to 180 days under Plan 1 and unlimited for Plans 2 and 3
- Skilled nursing care service up to 180 days during any calendar year. This benefit applies to all plans
- Non-custodial home health care services under each policy for 270 visits each calendar year, 20 percent coverage in-network, 40 percent out-of-network, not exceeding $150 for each day
- Second surgical opinion; this benefit is elective under Plan 1 and mandatory under Plans 2 and 3
- Prescription drug coverage
- Outpatient care/doctor visits
- Physical therapy

■ IOWA

Organization Administering Insurance and Contact:

A. Organization—Iowa Comprehensive Health Association (ICHA)
B. State contact—ICHA
   P.O. Box 33728, Indianapolis
   IN 46203-0728
   800-877-5156

Eligibility Criteria and Premium Cap:

The participant must be a resident of Iowa and have received from one or more insurers:

- Notice of rejection for substantially similar health insurance dated within the last nine months;
- Notice of benefit reduction or specific condition exclusion; and
- Notice of premium increase for similar coverage that exceeds the ICHA policy rate.

Coverage is also available to the resident who has been diagnosed with a condition listed on the plan brochure. In this instance, the above items do not have to be satisfied.

- An individual may also qualify if he or she is federally eligible.

Premium cap—The figure is capped at 150 percent of the standard rate for health insurance in the state.

Waiting Period for Pre-Existing Condition and Waiver of Waiting Period:

- *Waiting period*—Coverage is excluded during the six-month period following the effective date of coverage for any condition for which medical advice, care, or treatment was recommended or received during the six-month period immediately preceding enrollment.
- *Waiver of waiting period*—The waiting period is waived if (a) the pre-existing condition factor has been satisfied with the previous carrier, (b) the previous coverage was involuntarily terminated, (c) there was not a conversion policy offered with similar coverage and lower rates, and (d) application for the high-risk insurance is received within 63 days from the date the previous policy was canceled. Waiver is also granted if the applicant is federally eligible as of the date he or she seeks coverage.

Coverage:

The following types of plans are offered:

- *Plan Option A*
    - Annual deductible—$500 per insured
    - Out-of-pocket limit including deductible—$1,500 for an individual and $3,000 annual out-of-pocket met

- Co-insurance—20 percent
- Annual coverage after out-of-pocket met—100 percent
- Plan Option B
  - Annual deductible—$1,000 per insured
  - Out-of-pocket limit including deductible—$2,000 for an individual and $4,000 annual out-of-pocket met
  - Co-insurance—20 percent
  - Annual coverage after out-of-pocket met—100 percent
- Plan Option C
  - Annual deductible—$1,500 per insured
  - Out-of-pocket limit including deductible—$2,500 for an individual and $5,000 annual out-of-pocket met
  - Co-insurance—20 percent
  - Annual coverage after out-of-pocket met—100 percent
- Plan Option D
  - Annual deductible—$2,000 per insured
  - Out-of-pocket limit including deductible—$3,000 for an individual and $6,000 annual out-of-pocket met
  - Co-insurance—20 percent
  - Annual coverage after out-of-pocket met—100 percent

The Iowa plan includes the following services:

- Inpatient care/hospital—180 days semi-private room per calendar year
- Outpatient care/doctor visits
- Prescription drug coverage—100 percent covered after deductible is met for generic drugs
- Ambulance
- Skilled nursing care—180 days per calendar year
- Home health visits—180 days per calendar year
- Durable medical equipment
- Physical therapy

■ KANSAS

Organization Administering Insurance and Contact:

A. Organization—Kansas Uninsurable Health Insurance (KUHI)

B. State contact—Benefit Management, Inc.
2015-16th Street
Great Bend, KS 67530
800-290-1368

Eligibility Criteria and Premium Cap:

Participant must be eligible because of a medical condition or meet the standards prescribed for federal eligibility.

Medical Condition Eligibility:

- Applicant must have been a resident of Kansas for six months;
- Is ineligible for coverage under federal and state programs, including Medicaid or a group health plan; and
- Has been offered coverage at a rate higher than the KUHI plan; or
- Has been refused health coverage by two carriers because of health condition; or
- Has been involuntarily terminated from a health insurance plan for any reason other than non-payment of premium.

Premium cap—The statute establishing the Kansas Uninsurable Health Insurance Act provides that premium cap rates shall be reasonable in terms of the benefits provided, the risk experience, and the expenses of providing the coverage.

Waiting Period with Pre-Existing Condition and Waiver Waiting Period:

- *Waiting period*—Benefits are not covered for any pre-existing condition for the first 90 days following the effective date of coverage. A pre-existing condition is defined as any condition for which medical advice, care, or treatment was recommended or received from a medical practitioner as to such conditions during the six-month period proceeding the effective date of coverage.
- *Waiver of waiting period*—If covered under another policy that provides hospital, medical, or surgical benefits, and coverage under that policy terminates less than 31 days prior to coverage beginning under the plan, the 90-day period will be waived to the extent that the pre-existing condition limitation period was satisfied under the previous policy. A pre-existing condition waiting period does not apply to an insured who is federally eligible.

Coverage:

The insurance plan in Kansas is designed as a PPO with six deductibles, ranging from $500 to $7,500. The co-insurance is 70/30 for in-network expenses after the deductible is met, adjusted to 90/10 after payment of the annual maximum. Out-of-network payments are limited to 50 percent of the charge.

Coverage under the plan includes:

- Inpatient hospital expense—Daily room and board; semi-private room. Subject to deductible and co-insurance levels
- Outpatient care/doctor visits
- Prescription drug coverage—Outpatient paid at 50 percent after deductible is reached
- Ambulance—Ground and air when medically necessary
- Durable medical equipment—Subject to deductible and co-insurance levels
- Physical therapy—Subject to deductible and co-insurance levels
- Skilled nursing care—Subject to deductible and co-insurance levels
- Home health visits—Subject to deductible and co-insurance levels

■ KENTUCKY

Organization Administering Insurance and Contact:

A. Organization—Kentucky Access

B. State contact—Kentucky Access
P.O. Box 33707
Indianapolis, IN 46203-0707
866-405-6145

Eligibility Criteria and Premium Cap:

- Applicant must have been a resident of Kentucky for 12 months;
- Is ineligible for insurance providing comparable coverage; and
- Meets one of the following eligibility categories:
  - Has been refused health coverage by two carriers because of health condition; or
  - A diagnosis with a medical condition that automatically qualifies the applicant for Kentucky Access; or

- Has received notice of premium increase for similar coverage that exceeds the Kentucky Access policy rate.

An individual may also qualify if he or she is federally eligible.

Premium cap—150 percent for first year of coverage; 175 percent thereafter.

Waiting Period with Pre-Existing Condition and Waiver of Waiting Period:

- *Waiting period*—Benefits are not covered for any pre-existing condition for 12 months following the effective date of coverage. A pre-existing condition is defined as any condition for which medical advice, care, or treatment was recommended or received from a medical practitioner as to such conditions during the six-month period proceeding the effective date of coverage.

- *Waiver of waiting period*—A waiting period of 12 consecutive months will be reduced by the number of days the qualifying previous plan was in effect. A reduction in this waiting period is only allowed if there is no break in coverage of greater than 62 days between two plans.

Coverage:

Two PPO plans (Premier Access) and an indemnity plan (Traditional Access) are offered by the Kentucky Access program.

The indemnity plan provides a $400 individual and $800 family deductible. The individual deductible is subject to a maximum out-of-pocket payment of $1,500 after that deductible has been met. The family deductible is subject to a maximum out-of-pocket payment of $3,000 after that deductible has been met.

The PPOs offer a range of deductibles. In the more expensive of the two plans, the co-insurance ranges from 10 percent to 20 percent for in-network services and 35 percent to 40 percent for out-of-network care. In the other PPO, the in-network services range from 20 percent to 50 percent, and 40 percent to 50 percent for out-of-network care.

The coverage under the plan includes:

- Inpatient hospital expense—Daily room and board; semi-private room, subject to deductible and co-insurance levels
- Outpatient care/doctor visits
- Prescription drug coverage
- Ambulance
- Durable medical equipment
- Physical therapy
- Skilled nursing care
- Home health visits

◼ LOUISIANA

Organization Administering Insurance and Contact:

A. Organization—Louisiana Health Insurance Association

B. State contact—Louisiana Health Plan (LHP)
P.O. Drawer 83880
Baton Rouge, LA 70884-3880
225-926-6245
800-736-0947

Eligibility Criteria and Premium Cap:

There are three ways to become eligible for LHP:

- Federal eligibility.
- Involuntary loss of coverage requiring the participant to:
  - Have lost coverage involuntarily after being insured under major medical continuously and
  - Not have a break in coverage from the time the previous insurance was terminated of 63 or more days.
- Proof of uninsurability meeting the following criteria:
  - Louisiana resident for at least six months; and
  - Had application rejected within one year by two insurance companies; or
  - Had received notice of premium increase for similar coverage that is at least twice the LHP rate.

Premium cap—The figure is initially capped at 125 percent of the standard rate for comparable coverage. Thereafter, the premium may not exceed 200 percent of the standard rate.

Waiting Period with Pre-Existing Condition and Waiver of Waiting Period:

- *Waiting period for pre-existing conditions*—Coverage is excluded during the six-month period following the effective date of coverage for any condition for which medical advice, care, or treatment was recommended or received during the six-month period immediately preceding enrollment.
- *Waiver of waiting period*—Full or partial waiver of waiting period is offered to those individuals who had qualifying previous coverage that had been terminated no more than 63 days prior to the LHP coverage. Individuals who are federally eligible are not subject to a waiting period.

Coverage:

Louisiana only offers individual PPO plans with deductibles at $1,000 (Plan J), $2,000 (Plan K), $3,500 (Plan L), and $5,000 (Plan M). The co-insurance is generally 75/25 for provider services. The coverage under the plan includes:

- Out-of-pocket maximum—Varies by plan, ranging from $1,500 to $4,500
- Inpatient hospital expense
- Outpatient care/doctor visits
- Prescription drug coverage—Brand at 70 percent coverage, generic at 80 percent coverage, and mail order at 90 percent coverage. $15,000 per calendar year maximum
- Ambulance
- Skilled nursing care—Limited to 120 days per calendar year
- Home health visits—Limited to 270 days per calendar year

■ MINNESOTA

Organization Administering Insurance and Contact:

A. Organization—Minnesota Comprehensive Health Association (MCHA)

B. State contact—Minnesota Comprehensive Health Association
5775 Wayzata Blvd., Suite 910
St. Louis Park, MN 55416
952-593-9609

Eligibility Criteria and Premium Cap:

A participant must:

- Be a resident of Minnesota for six months and
- Have been refused health coverage; or
- Offered coverage at a higher than standard premium; or
- Have been offered health coverage with a restrictive rider or pre-existing conditions limitation that reduces coverage. At least one insurer must have provided this within six months prior to the date of enrollment.

In addition, any resident who has been treated within the last three years for one of the presumptive conditions approved by the Minnesota Department of Commerce is automatically eligible for coverage.

Individuals are also eligible if they meet the standards for federal eligibility.

Premium cap—The cap is 125 percent of the weighted average of rates charged by a majority of the insurers and HMOs offering similar coverage.

Waiting Period with Pre-Existing Condition and Waiver of Waiting Period:

- *Waiting period*—Coverage is excluded during the six-month period following the effective date of coverage for any condition for which medical advice, care, or treatment was recommended or received during the six-month period immediately preceding enrollment.
- *Waiver of waiting period*—Full or partial waiver of waiting period is offered to those individuals who had qualifying previous coverage that had been terminated no more than 90 days prior to the LHP coverage. Individuals who are federally eligible are not subject to a waiting period.

Coverage:

The following types of plans are offered:

- *Qualified Plan One*
  - Annual deductible—$1,000 per insured
  - Coverage after deductible—80 percent until $3,000 annual out-of-pocket met
  - Annual coverage after out-of-pocket met—100 percent
- *Qualified Plan Two*
  - Annual deductible—$500 per insured
  - Coverage after deductible—80 percent until $3,000 annual out-of-pocket met
  - Annual coverage after out-of-pocket met—100 percent
- *Extended Basic Medicare Supplement*
  - Coverage—Part A and B expenses
  - Prescription drugs and other benefits mandated by state law—80 percent
- *Basic Medicare Supplement Plan*
  - Coverage—Limited coverage for Parts A and B
  - Not covered—Parts A and B deductibles and prescription drugs. Riders, however, may be purchased for coverage of A and B deductibles and 80 percent of usual and customary costs.

The benefits provided under the four Minnesota plans include:

- Hospital services
- Professional services for the diagnosis or treatment of injuries, illnesses, or conditions

- Prescription drug coverage; for coverage under the Medicare policies, limited prescription drugs are only included in the Extended Plan
- Services of a nursing home for not more than 120 days, provided that the services qualify under Medicare
- Services of a home health agency if the services would qualify under Medicare
- Opinion of a second physician on surgical procedures
- Outpatient doctor visits
- Physical therapy

■ MISSISSIPPI

Organization Administering Insurance and Contact:

A. Organization—Mississippi Comprehensive Health Insurance Risk Pool Association (MCHIRP)

B. State contact—Comprehensive Health Insurance Risk Pool Association
P.O. Box 13748
Jackson, MS 39236
601-362-0799
888-820-9400

Eligibility Criteria and Premium Cap:

There are two ways to become eligible.

Federal Eligibility

For individuals who are not federally eligible, the following standards must be met:

- Participants must be a legal resident of the state for six months and
- Have an automatically rejectable health condition; or
- During the 12 months preceding application, have been rejected by one insurer; or
- Offered a policy which is substantially similar to the high-risk plan at a premium in excess of that insurance; or
- Were previously enrolled in another state's high-risk insurance pool.

Premium cap—The cap for the first year of the policy may not exceed 150 percent of the standard rate. For future years, this figure may increase to 175 percent of the standard rate.

Waiting Period for Pre-Existing Condition and Waiver of Waiting Period:

- *Waiting period and pre-existing conditions*—Coverage is excluded during a six-month period following the effective date of coverage for any condition for which diagnosis, care, or treatment was recommended or received during the six months immediately preceding enrollment medical advice.

- *Waiver of waiting period*—MCHIRP will limit its exclusion in treating a pre-existing condition to three months if the insured was covered under another policy that was terminated for a reason other than his or her fault. A pre-existing condition waiting period also does not apply to an insured who is federally eligible.

Coverage:

The Mississippi Risk Pool Plan is a major medical plan that offers deductibles of $1,000 Medical/$250 Pharmacy or $2,000 Medical/$500 Pharmacy. Benefits are generally covered on an 80/20 co-pay basis and there is no limit on out-of-pocket amount under the plan. Benefits include:

- Outpatient/doctor visits
- Inpatient care/hospital services
- Prescription drug coverage—Non-preferred name at 50 percent of allowable charge; brand names at 80 percent of allowable charge; and generic drugs at 100 percent of allowable charge
- Skilled nursing care—Private duty nursing is limited to $5,000 per calendar year with an aggregate lifetime limit of $20,000
- Home health visits—Considered on an individual basis
- Physical therapy—$5,000 per calendar year with a lifetime maximum of $20,000
- Durable medical equipment—80 percent limited to $5,000 per calendar year with a lifetime maximum of $20,000

■ MISSOURI

Organization Administering Insurance and Contact:

A. Organization—Missouri Health Insurance Pool

B. State contact—Missouri Health Insurance Pool
   1831 Chestnut Street
   St. Louis, MO 63103
   314-923-4444

(For individuals residing in Kansas City, MO, or adjacent counties, the address to contact is P.O. Box 8966, Kansas City, MO 64114, and the telephone number is 800-821-2231.)

Eligibility Criteria and Premium Cap:

- Must be a resident of the state;
- Is not insured unless the plan charges premiums in excess of 300 percent of the standard rate for comparable insurance;
- Is not eligible for Part A and Part B of Medicare;
- Is not receiving benefits under Medicaid or a Medical Assistance Program;
- Has not been refused insurance because of an alcohol or substance abuse conviction or self-inflicted injury; and
- Was involuntarily terminated from his or her health insurance coverage for reasons other than non-payment of premium or fraud; or
- Has been refused health coverage or offered coverage at a premium 300 percent of the standard rate; or
- Has been offered health coverage with a restrictive rider substantially limiting coverage.

Premium cap—The cap may not be less than 150 percent or more than 200 percent of the standard rate.

Waiting Period with Pre-Existing Condition and Waiver of Waiting Period:

- *Waiting period*—Coverage is excluded during the first 12 months following the effective date of coverage for any condition for which medical care, diagnosis, or advice was recommended or received or should have been sought by an ordinarily prudent person during the six-month period immediately preceding the effective date of coverage.
- *Waiver of waiting period*—There is a waiver of the waiting period if it has already been satisfied under any prior coverage for which coverage was involuntarily terminated, and if applied within 60 days or if conversion rates are 300 percent of the standard rate set by the pool.

Coverage:

The plan offered is structured as a PPO with a co-insurance of 20 percent for in-network provider services and 50 percent for out-of-network provider services. The following summarizes the deductible amounts offered with corresponding out-of-pocket maximums:

	Plan I	Plan II	Plan III	Plan IV
In-Network Deductible	$500 per year	$1,000 per year	$2,500 per year	$5,000 per year
Out-of-Network Deductible	$1,000 per year	$2,000 per year	$5,000 per year	$10,000 per year
Out-of-Pocket Maximums*	$2,500 per year + deductible	$5,000 per year + deductible	$5,000 per year + deductible	$5,000 per year + deductible

* The maximum applies only to services received by in-network providers.

Benefits include:

- Outpatient care/doctor visits
- Inpatient care/hospital including surgery
- Prescription drug coverage
- Skilled nursing care (limited to 30 days per calendar year)
- Home health visits (limited to 20 visits per calendar year)
- Physical therapy

■ MONTANA

Organization Administering Insurance and Contact:

A. Organization—Montana Comprehensive Health Association

B. State contact—Montana Comprehensive Health Association
c/o Blue Cross and Blue Shield of Montana
560 N. Park Avenue
Helena, MT 59604
406-444-8537

Eligibility Criteria:

An individual is eligible if he or she meets the following criteria:

- Is a resident of the state and
- Has received one of the following by at least two insurers within six months prior to application:
  - Rejection for disability or health insurance; or
  - A restrictive rider or pre-existing condition limitation; or

- Has a specified major illness, and
- Is not eligible for any other health insurance coverage.

An individual also qualifies by meeting the standards of federal eligibility.

Premium cap—The Board of the Montana Comprehensive Health Association has set the premium cap at 200 percent of the average of top five insurers of individual plans.

Waiting Period with Pre-Existing Condition and Waiver of Waiting Period:
- *Waiting period*—Benefits are not covered for any pre-existing condition for 12 months following the effective date of coverage. A pre-existing condition is defined as any condition for which medical advice, care, or treatment was recommended or received from a medical practitioner as to such conditions during the five-year period proceeding the effective date of coverage.
- *Waiver of waiting period*—Waiting period does not apply to newborn children or children placed for adoption. Otherwise, creditable coverage will apply if:
  - Applicant did not voluntarily cancel coverage;
  - Application was made within 30 days of the most recent coverage; and
  - All other options for insurance (including COBRA) have been exhausted.

There is no waiting period for applicants who meet the standards set for federal eligibility.

Coverage:
If the applicant is federally eligible, he or she will have the choice of two portability plans and the Traditional plan. Otherwise, only the Traditional plan is available.

The Traditional plan is structured as a PPO with a co-payment of 20 percent and a deductible of $1,000 with a maximum out-of-pocket including the deductible—of $5,000.

Benefits include:

- Hospital services
- Physician services
- Physical therapy
- Ambulance services
- Durable medical equipment
- Home health care (up to 180 visits per benefit period)
- Services of a convalescent home as an alternative to hospital services—Maximum of 60 days

- Prescription drug coverage which provides a 20 percent co-pay for generic, 30 percent co-pay for brand named formulary, and 40 percent co-pay for brand name non-formulary; there is no deductible, with a maximum of $2,000 per year

■ NEBRASKA

Organization Administering Insurance and Contact:

A. Organization—Nebraska Comprehensive Health Insurance Pool (CHIP)

B. State contact—Nebraska Comprehensive Health Association
Blue Cross and Blue Shield of Nebraska
P.O. Box 3248
Main Post Office
Omaha, NE 68180-0001
402-343-3337

Eligibility Criteria and Premium Cap:

Participant must:

- Be a resident of the state for at least six-months and
- Have been rejected for health insurance coverage within the last six months from an insurer licensed in Nebraska for medical reasons; or
- Offered, within six months prior to application, health insurance subject to a restrictive rider limiting coverage for a pre-existing medical condition; or
- Offered coverage at a rate exceeding the premium rate for pool coverage.

Having a diagnosis of one of several specified medical conditions automatically qualifies the applicant for coverage.

Premium cap—The Nebraska Comprehensive Health Insurance Pool has set the premium cap at 135 percent of the rate for comparable coverage.

Waiting Period With Pre-Existing Condition and Waiver of Waiting Period:

- *Waiting period*—Charges and expenses listed as a benefit in the policy will not be allowed if incurred during the first six months following the effective date of coverage as to any condition that has manifested itself or for which medical advice, care, or treatment was recommended or received during the six-month period preceding coverage.
- *Waiver of waiting period*—A person is eligible for a waiver/credit if his or her health coverage was involuntarily terminated after January 1, 1992. The person

must be eligible for the coverage offered by the high-risk pool and apply for the pre-existing waiver within 60 days after involuntary termination. In addition, the applicant cannot be eligible for a conversion policy or continuation of coverage under federal law. An individual who is federally eligible will not be subject to a waiting period.

The six months' pre-existing condition is also waived if the participant had been insured under a conversion or COBRA policy. To be eligible for coverage, the insured must have applied for this coverage within 90 days of the termination of the conversion or COBRA policy, and termination must have been for a reason other than non-payment of the premium.

Coverage:

The Comprehensive Health Insurance Pool offers two plans—a PPO and a Major Medical.

The PPO has a selection of four deductible amounts ($250/$500/$1,000 and $2,000) with co-insurance of 20 percent for in-network charges and 30 percent for out-of network charges.

The Major Medical has the same deductibles as offered in the PPO with a co-insurance of 20 percent.

The coverage is the same for both plans except for prescription drugs. Under the PPO policy, there is a $10 co-payment for most covered prescriptions purchased at a participating pharmacy. Under the Major Medical Plan, generic drugs are payable at 100 percent and brand name prescriptions at 80 percent.

Coverage offered in both plans include:

- Hospital room and board
- Physician service
- Physical and speech therapy
- X-ray and laboratory exams
- Medical supplies
- Prescription drugs
- Home health care
- Skilled nursing care

NEW MEXICO

Organization Administering Insurance and Contact:

A. Organization—New Mexico Medical Insurance Pool (NMMIP)

B. State contact—New Mexico Blue Cross and Blue Shield
P.O. Box 27630
Albuquerque, NM 87125-7630
800-432-0750
505-292-2600

Eligibility Criteria and Premium Cap:

Participant must be a resident of New Mexico and

- Have received notice of rejection of coverage for substantially similar health insurance; or
- Have received notice that the rate applied to his or her coverage will exceed the premiums imposed on the comprehensive insurance as to its $500 deductible plan; or
- Have received a notice of reduction or limitation of coverage, including a restrictive rider that excludes benefits for a condition for longer than 12 months that is specific to the applicant; or
- Have lost coverage from an individual plan due to the insurer having stopped offering such coverage or because it no longer sells health insurance in New Mexico.

A resident is also eligible if he or she meets the criteria for federal eligibility.

Premium cap—The figure is capped at 125 percent of the standard rate for comparable coverage.

Waiting Period with Pre-existing Conditions and Waiver of Waiting Period:

- *Waiting period*—The coverage under the comprehensive insurance plan excludes charges or expenses incurred during the first six months following the effective date of coverage if the condition manifested itself or if medical advice, care, or treatment was recommended or received within six months preceding the effective date of coverage.

- *Waiver of waiting period*—The waiting period is waived if similar exclusions have been satisfied under any prior health insurance coverage that was involuntarily terminated and the application for comprehensive coverage is made within 31 days following the involuntary termination. In that case, such coverage will be effective from the date the prior coverage was terminated. Individuals who are federally eligible are not subject to a waiting period.

Coverage:

NMMIP provides four plans, each with a different deductible and out-of-pocket maximum. The following summarizes the plans offered:

	Plan I	Plan II	Plan III	Plan IV
Deductible/person	$500 per year	$1,000 per year	$2,000 per year	$7,500 per year
Out-of-pocket maximums/ individual	$2,500 per year (includes deductible and coinsurance)	$3,500 per year (includes deductible and coinsurance)	$5,000 per year (includes deductible and coinsurance)	N/A
Out-of-pocket maximums/family	$5,000 per year (includes deductible and coinsurance)	$7,000 per year (includes deductible and coinsurance)	$10,000 per year (includes deductible and coinsurance)	N/A
% paid after payment of deductible but before out-of-pocket maximum is reached	80%	80%	80 %	N/A
% paid after out-of-pocket maximum is reached	100%	100%	100%	N/A

Benefits include:

- Hospital room and board
- Basic medical and surgical services
- Professional services provided by a physician for the treatment or diagnosis of an illness or injury
- Rental or purchase of durable medical equipment
- Private duty nursing service (limited to $10,000 of covered expenses per person per calendar year)
- Prescription drugs (subject to a 25 percent per prescription co-payment)
- Skilled nursing facility services up to 100 days per person per calendar year
- Home health visits—100 medically necessary visits per year from a licensed home health agency
- Physical therapy

NORTH DAKOTA

Organization Administering Insurance and Contact:

A. Organization—Comprehensive Health Association of North Dakota (CHAND)

B. State contact—Administrative Board
Blue Cross and Blue Shield of North Dakota
4510 13th Avenue SW
Fargo, ND 58121-0001
800-737-0016
701-277-2271

Eligibility Criteria and Premium Cap:

Participant must:

- Have been a resident of the State of North Dakota continuously for six months;
- Be under the age of 65; and
- Within the last six months have
    - Written evidence of rejection by one insurer or
    - Have been offered coverage by an insurer that is subject to a rider substantially restricting benefits for specific conditions.

A resident is also eligible if he or she meets the criteria for federal eligibility.

Premium cap—The premium may not exceed 135 percent of the standard rate for comparable coverage.

Waiting Period with Pre-Existing Condition and Waiver of Waiting Period:

- *Waiting period*—Coverage will not be provided for services, supplies, or charges received during the first 180 days of the policy (270 days for maternity benefits) for the treatment of any pre-existing condition that was diagnosed or treated within 90 days prior to the effective date of the policy.
- *Waiver of waiting period*—A waiting period of 180 consecutive days will be reduced by the number of days the qualifying previous plan was in effect. A reduction in this waiting period is only allowed if there is no break in coverage of greater than 62 days between the two plans. Applicants who are federally eligible are not subject to a waiting period.

Coverage:

The plan offered is structured as a medical plan with a co-payment of 20 percent after the deductible is met. The deductibles offered are $500 and $1,000. The co-insurance maximum for the calendar year for the plan offering a $500 deductible is

$2,500; the plan subject to a $1,000 deductible has a co-insurance maximum of $2,000. Once the out-of-pocket amount exceeds $3,000 for either plan (deductible + co-insurance), the benefit amount for covered services for the remainder of the calendar year is 100 percent.

The services offered under the CHAND plan include:

- Hospitalization and in-hospital medical care
- Surgical services
- Physical therapy—Maximum benefit of 90 days per condition
- Outpatient care/doctor visits—Deductible waived
- Prescription drug coverage
- Skilled nursing services when admission occurs within 14 days of a prior hospital stay of at least three days; limited to 120 days of inpatient per year
- Chiropractic services—Limitations apply
- Home health visits—Maximum benefit of 180 visits per benefit period
- Rental or purchase of durable medical equipment

■ OKLAHOMA

Organization Administering Insurance and Contact:

A. Organization—Oklahoma Health Insurance High Risk Pool (OHRP)

B. State contact—OHRP
P.O. Box 50429
Midwest City, OK 73140-5429
405-741-8434

Eligibility Criteria and Premium Cap:

- *Medical Eligibility Program*—An individual applying for coverage under the Medical Eligibility Program must meet the following criteria:
  - Be a legal resident of Oklahoma for a period of at least 12 months;
  - Have been rejected by two insurers for coverage substantially similar to the high-risk insurance offered in the state because of a health condition;
  - Have been accepted for health insurance that excludes coverage for the insured's pre-existing condition;
  - Have been quoted an individual policy rate substantially higher than the OHRP rate; or
  - Have a specified major illness.

The comprehensive plan does not cover individuals who are under an employer-sponsored or self-insured plan. It also will not cover those who currently receive health care benefits under any federal or state program providing financial assistance and those who are eligible for either Medicare or Medicaid.

- *Federal eligibility*—A resident is also eligible if he or she meets the criteria for federal eligibility:
- *Premium cap*—The cap has been set at 150 percent of the average standard rate for comparable coverage.

Waiting Period with Pre-Existing Condition and Waiver of Waiting Period:

- *Waiting period*—A high-risk policy may contain provisions excluding coverage during a period of 12 months following the effective date of the policy as to a participant's pre-existing condition, as long as
  - The condition manifested itself within a period of six months before the effective date of coverage; or
  - Medical advice or treatment for the condition was recommended or received within a period of six months before the effective date of coverage.
- *Waiver of waiting period*—The 12-month waiting period will be waived if the participant was covered under another policy that provided hospital, medical, or surgical benefits, and coverage under that policy terminated less than 63 days prior to coverage beginning under the OHRP policy. Individuals who are federally eligible are not subject to a waiting period.

Coverage:

The plan offered is structured as a PPO with a co-payment of 20 percent of allowable charges for in-network provider services and 40 percent of allowable charges for out-of-network provider services. Six deductibles are offered, ranging from $500 to $7,500.

Coverage includes:

- Hospital services
- Professional services for the diagnosis and treatment of injuries, illnesses, or conditions other than dental
- Prescription drug coverage—Prescription drugs must be purchased at a designated network pharmacy, and are subject to the following co-pays:
  - $10 for generic drugs;
  - $20 for preferred drugs; and
  - $30 or 30 percent of drug cost (whichever is higher) for non-preferred drugs

- Services of a home health agency, provided that the services are of the type reimbursable by Medicare
- Nursing facility services (limited to 180 calendar days during a policy year)
- Physical therapy

■ OREGON

Organization Administering Insurance and Contact:

A. Organization—Oregon Medical Insurance Pool (OMIP)

B. State contact—Oregon Medical Insurance Pool
250 Church Street SE
Suite 200
Salem, OR 97301-3921
503-373-1692

Eligibility Criteria and Premium Cap:

An applicant must satisfy either of the following:

- *Medical Eligibility Standard (OMIP portable plan):*
    - Had been covered under a self-insured group plan for at least six months and applied for the high-risk plan within 63 days of losing coverage; or
    - Had health coverage from another state high-risk insurance pool and applied for OMIP within 63 days of losing coverage; and
    - Is a resident of the state. If the criteria are not met, a resident is still eligible, provided he or she is not Medicare eligible and refused individual insurance due to his or her health status.
- *Federal Eligibility Standard*—A resident is also eligible if he or she meets federal eligibility.
- *Premium cap*—The premium is initially set at 125 percent of the standard rate for comparable coverage.

Waiting Period with Pre-Existing Conditions and Waiver of Waiting Period:

- *Waiting period*—Pre-existing conditions will not be covered for the first six months of enrollment unless credit is granted toward the waiting period.
- *Waiver of waiting period*—A participant may receive credit toward the waiting period if he or she had prior health coverage, was involuntarily terminated, and an application for OMIP was made within 60 days of termination. Individuals who are federally eligible are not subject to a waiting period.

Coverage:

Oregon has four different plans, two indemnity plans (a traditional plan and a low cost/limited benefit plan), a PPO, and a managed care plan. All four plans offer similar benefits, but pay benefits at different rates in the event the provider networks are not used. If the participant is enrolled in the PPO and uses a non-network provider, the plan pays 60 percent and not 80 percent. If the participant is enrolled in the managed care plan and uses a non-network provider, the plan pays nothing toward the claim.

Benefits provided under the plans include:

- Hospitalization—80 percent for indemnity and PPO; 80 percent after $200 co-payment per admission for managed care plan; the low cost-limited benefit pays 70 percent
- Doctor visits—80 percent for indemnity and PPO; 100 percent after $15 co-payment if primary care physician and 80 percent if specialist or hospital visit for managed care plan; the low cost plan pays 70 percent
- Skilled nursing care (in home)—80 percent up to 60 visits per calendar year except for the low cost plan, which pays 70 percent
- Prescription drugs—80 percent payment for the indemnity and PPO; 80 percent as well for the managed care plan if a participating pharmacy is used, 50 percent for a non-participating pharmacy
- Other benefits:
  - Ambulance
  - Rental or purchase of durable medical equipment
  - Emergency room
  - Physical therapy
  - Surgery

The low-cost limited benefit plan is a state program in which a policy is subsidized for qualified state residents who were previously uninsured. Subsidies are provided at different percentages based on the applicant's income.

■ SOUTH CAROLINA

Organization Administering Insurance and Contact:

A. Organization—South Carolina Health Insurance Pool

B. State contact—Blue Cross and Blue Shield of South Carolina
P.O. Box 61173
Columbia, SC 29260-1173
800-868-2500, ext. 42757

Eligibility Criteria and Premium Cap:

Participant must be a resident of South Carolina for 30 days and have experienced any of the following:

- Refusal to issue health insurance by any insurer for health reasons;
- Refusal to issue insurance except with a reduction of coverage for a pre-existing condition exceeding 12 months;
- Refusal to issue comparable insurance coverage except at a rate exceeding 150 percent of the pool rate.

An individual may also qualify for coverage if he or she meets the standards of federal eligibility.

Premium cap—The premium charged may not exceed 200 percent of the standard rate for comparable coverage.

Waiting Period with Pre-Existing Condition and Waiver of Waiting Period:

- *Waiting period*—Coverage under the plan excludes charges incurred during the first six months following the effective date of coverage as to any condition which, during the six-month period immediately preceding the effective date of coverage (a) had manifested itself in such a manner as would cause an ordinarily prudent person to seek diagnosis, care, or treatment or (b) for which medical care, advice, or treatment was recommended or received as to the condition.
- *Waiver of waiting period*—Waiver is effective if satisfied under the previous insurance for which coverage was involuntarily terminated or if the applicant is federally eligible.

Coverage:

South Carolina offers two plans, an in-network plan and a comprehensive policy.

The in-network plan requires a 20 percent co-payment for in-network provider charges and 40 percent for out-of-network provider charges plus any amounts above the allowable charges. The co-payment for the comprehensive coverage is 20 percent plus any amounts above the allowable charges. The deductible imposed in both plans is $500.

The plans differ in the annual maximum that must be paid by the insured.

The comprehensive plan has an annual maximum of $1,500, whereas the PPO has an annual maximum of $2,000 for in-network providers and $7,000 for services that are out-of-network.

The benefits provided in the plans include:

- Inpatient hospital expense

- Outpatient care/doctor visits (after deductible is met)
- Surgery
- Home health visits (up to 40 days per benefit period)
- Prescription drug coverage (80 percent after deductible)
- Physical therapy
- Durable medical equipment

■ TENNESSEE

Organization Administering Insurance and Contact:
A. Organization—TennCare Select
B. State contact—Bureau of TennCare
   P.O. Box 22630
   Nashville, TN 37202-2630
   800-669-1851

Eligibility Criteria and Premium Cap:
The program, referred to as TennCare Select, provides coverage to those individuals considered "uninsurable" and to those who do not have access to an employer-sponsored health plan. A participant must:

- Be a U.S. citizen or a legal resident alien;
- Reside in the State of Tennessee;
- Provide a verified Social Security number; and
- Not be an inmate of a correctional facility.

Premium cap—The premium cap is based on the size of the participant's household and that individual's monthly income.

Waiting Period for Pre-Existing Condition and Waiver of Waiting Period:
- *Waiting period*—There is no waiting period.
- *Waiver of waiting period*—Not applicable.

Coverage:
The basic medical plan includes hospital, outpatient hospital, prescriptive drugs, durable equipment, physical therapy, and physician and specialist office visits. The plan provides preventive care by requiring early and periodic screening without the requirements of co-payments and deductibles.

When the deductible is applicable, the amount per participant is $250 annually and $500 annually for a family. The amount or rate of co-payment is based on the participant's income.

■ TEXAS

Organization Administering Insurance and Contact:
A. Organization—Texas Health Insurance Risk Pool
B. State contact—Texas Health Insurance Risk Pool
   2512 South IH-35 #110
   Austin, TX 78704
   512-441-7665

Eligibility Criteria and Premium Cap:

An individual (including dependents of the insured) is eligible for high-risk insurance if he or she is under the age of 65, a legal resident of Texas for at least 30 days, a United States citizen or a permanent resident of the United States for at least three continuous years, and provides evidence of one of the following:

- Notice of rejection or refusal by an insurance company to issue substantially similar health coverage to the individual due to health reasons;
- An offer by an insurer or HMO to issue individual health coverage, providing substantially similar coverage at a premium rate greater than the current Health Pool rate;
- Diagnosis as having one of a series of illnesses;
- Certification from a salaried representative of an insurance company or agent that they are unable to obtain substantially similar individual coverage because of the applicant's medical condition; or
- An offer by either an HMO or an insurer to issue a policy that excludes a medical condition or conditions.

An individual may also qualify for coverage if he or she meets standards of federal eligibility.

Premium cap—First year premium cap of between 125 percent and 150 percent of the standard rate for comparable individual health insurance and 200 percent of the standard rate for renewal years. The Board of Directors set the 2002 rates at 165 percent of the standard rate.

Waiting Period for Pre-Existing Condition and Waiver of Waiting Period:

- *Waiting period*—Coverage is excluded during a 12-month period following the effective date of coverage for any condition for which medical advice, care, or treatment was recommended or received during the six months immediately preceding enrollment.

- *Waiver of waiting period*—The pre-existing condition limitation does not apply if an individual was continuously covered for a period of 12 months under other health coverage that was in effect up to a date not more than 63 days before the participant's effective date of coverage through the Health Pool. Credit is given for the time the insured was covered under any prior health insurance that was in effect at any time during the 12-month period before the effective date of Health Pool coverage. Individuals who are federally eligible are not subject to a waiting period.

Coverage:

Texas offers a comprehensive major medical plan in which the co-insurance for network services is 20 percent and 40 percent for non-network services. There is an option of three deductibles that may be selected by the applicant; $500, $1,000, and $2,500. The co-insurance maximums for PPO providers are $2,000, $3,000, and $7,500, respectively. The benefits provided in the plan include:

- Inpatient hospital expense and outpatient care/doctor visits
- Prescription drugs that may be purchased at a PPO pharmacy ($10 co-payment for generic drugs/$25 co-payment for preferred brand name drugs/$40 co-payment for non-preferred brand name drugs), a non-PPO pharmacy (insured pays 40 percent of the average wholesale price plus dispensing fee)
- Home health care (120 visits per calendar year)
- Skilled nursing facility (120 days per calendar year)
- Physical therapy

UTAH

Organization Administering Insurance and Contact:

A. Organization—Utah Comprehensive Health Insurance Pool (UCHIP)

B. State contact—UCHIP
P.O. Box 30270
Salt Lake City, UT 84130
801-333-5573

Eligibility:

An individual is eligible for the insurance offered by UCHIP if he or she meets the following criteria:

- Has resided in Utah for at least 12 months;
- Pays the established premium;
- Applied for comprehensive health coverage not more than 30 days after he or she is denied coverage by a private individual insurer;
- In the event of termination of a similar type of insurance from another state because the applicant is now a resident of Utah, has applied for the UCHIP policy within 31 days from the date of cancellation.

An individual may also qualify for coverage if he or she meets standards of federal eligibility.

Waiting Period for Pre-Existing Condition, and Waiver of Waiting Period:

- *Waiting period*—Coverage is excluded during a six-month period following the effective date of the insurance for any condition for which diagnostic care or treatment was recommended or received during the six-month period immediately preceding enrollment.
- *Waiver of waiting period*—A waiver is effective if the individual applies for an HIP plan within 31 days of losing his or her prior coverage. If the previous insurance was from another state high-risk pool, the application period is extended to 63 days. Individuals who are federally eligible are not subject to a waiting period.

Coverage:

Utah offers a medical indemnity policy with a co-insurance of 20 percent. There is an option of two deductibles that may be selected by the applicant—$500 and $1,000. If the $500 deductible is selected, the maximum out-of-pocket amount is $1,500. If the $1,000 deductible is selected, the maximum out-of-pocket amount is $2,000.

The basic plan includes the following services:

- Inpatient hospital services—80 percent after deductible
- Outpatient care/doctor services—80 percent after deductible
- Physical therapy—Prior approval required for more than five sessions
- Prescription drugs—80 percent after deductible
- Durable medical equipment—With prior approval, 80/20
- Home health services—Prior approval required; 80/20

- Medical supplies
- Laboratory, radiological, and other diagnostic tests

■ WASHINGTON

Organization Administering Insurance and Contact:

A. Organization—Washington State Health Insurance Pool (WSHIP)
B. State contact—WSHIP
 P.O. Box 33727
 Indianapolis, IN 46203-0727
 800-877-5187

Eligibility Criteria and Premium Cap:

Applicant must:

- Be a resident of the State of Washington; and
- Have proof of rejection for health insurance for medical reasons; or
- Reside in a county in Washington State in which commercial individual medical insurance is not available to residents; or
- In the case of a Medicare-eligible applicant, have one of the following:
  - Health insurance with a restrictive rider;
  - Health insurance with a pre-existing condition limitation; or
  - Health insurance with an up-rated premium.

An individual may also qualify for coverage if he or she meets the standards of federal eligibility.

Premium cap—The premium may not exceed 150 percent of the standard rate for comparable insurance except in the case of a managed care policy, when the premium cannot exceed 125 percent of the standard rate.

Waiting Period for Pre-Existing Condition and Waiver of Waiting Period:

- *Waiting period*—Coverage is excluded during a period of six months following the effective date of coverage for a condition for which medical advice, care, or treatment was recommended or received during the six months preceding enrollment.
- *Waiver of waiting period*—Pre-existing conditions will be waived if similar exclusions have been satisfied under any prior health insurance, provided that such

coverage had been terminated no more than 63 days from the date the individual applies for WSHIP. Individuals who are federally eligible are not subject to a waiting period.

Coverage:
- *Plan One*—A standard indemnity plan with deductibles of $500, $1,000, or $1,500. After the deductible has been met, the policy pays 80 percent of the covered charge until the out-of-pocket limitation has been satisfied for the plan year. 100 percent of the covered charge will then be paid for the remainder of the plan year.
- *Plan Two*—Medicare Eligible Plan for persons enrolled in Parts A and B. The plan is not subject to an annual deduction.
- *Plan Three*—Preferred Provider Plan with a choice of a $500 or $1,000 deductible. Until the out-of-pocket limit is reached, the plan pays 80 percent of network-covered charges and 60 percent of out-of-network covered expenses.

The benefits in the plans include:

- Semi-private hospital room and board and any other hospital services and supplies up to 180 days during the calendar year
- Professional services including surgery and treatment of injuries
- Prescription drugs
- Home health services and skilled nursing care—100 days per calendar year for each service
- Physical therapy
- Durable medical equipment
- Diagnostic X-ray and ambulance

■ WISCONSIN

Organization Administering Insurance and Contact:

A. Organization—Wisconsin Health Insurance Risk Sharing Plan (HIRSP)

B. State contact—HIRSP
   6406 Bridge Road
   Suite 18
   Madison, WI 53784
   800-828-4777

Eligibility Criteria and Premium Cap:

Participants must:

- Be a resident of Wisconsin for a period of at least 30 days;
- Be under the age of 65; and
- Have received one of the following within six months prior to application:
  - Notice of rejection or cancellation from one or more health insurers;
  - Notice of a reduction or limitation in health insurance coverage that substantially reduces coverage when compared to coverage available to persons considered standard risks;
  - Notice of an increase in a health insurance premium that exceeds the premium then in effect for the insured person by 50 percent or more, unless the increase applies to substantially all of the insurer's health policies then in effect; or
  - Notice of premium rate increase for health insurance applied for but not yet in effect. (This notice must be from one or more insurers and again be exceeded by at least 50 percent.)

An individual is also eligible if he or she meets the criteria for federal eligibility.

Premium cap—The cap is 200 percent of the standard rate for comparable health insurance.

Waiting Period for Pre-Existing Condition and Waiver of Waiting Period:

- *Waiting period*—Conditions diagnosed or treated in the six months preceding the policy date will not be covered for the first six months that a participant is covered by the plan.
- *Waiver of waiting period*—Pre-existing conditions will be waived if similar exclusions have been satisfied under any prior health insurance, provided that such coverage had been terminated no more than 63 days from the date the individual applies for HIRSP. Individuals who are federally eligible are not subject to a waiting period.

Coverage:

Wisconsin offers the following two plans:

- *Plan 1*—This plan is for individuals who are not Medicare eligible and provides the insured a choice of either a $1,000 or $2,500 deductible with an annual out-of-pocket maximum of $2,000 or $3,500 respectively. After the deductible is met, but before the out-of-pocket maximum is reached, the insurer is responsible for 80 percent of the covered charge. Once the maximum amount is reached, the insurer is responsible to pay 100 percent of the covered expense.

- *Plan 2*—This plan is for individuals who are Medicare eligible. The insurance is subject to an annual $500 deductible and the insured is not required to pay any co-insurance.

Both plans offer the following coverage:

- Hospital services
- Basic medical/surgical services
- Prescription drugs (drug card program, pharmacy network)
- Skilled nursing care (up to 30 days of care upon the specific recommendation and supervision of a physician)
- Home health visits (40 visits per year)
- Physical therapy
- Diagnostic/X-ray

■ WYOMING

Organization Administering Insurance and Contact:

A. Organization—Wyoming Health Insurance Pool

B. State contact—Wyoming Health Insurance Pool
4000 House Avenue
P.O. Box 2419
Cheyenne, WY 82003
307-634-1393

Eligibility Criteria and Premium Cap:

Participant must be a resident of the state and have proof of:

- Rejection or refusal to issue health insurance for health reasons by one insurer;
- Refusal to issue health insurance except at a rate exceeding the pool rate; or
- Refusal to issue health insurance except with a reduction or exclusion of coverage for a pre-existing condition for which reduction or exclusion is more restrictive than that provided by the pool.

An individual may also qualify for coverage if he or she meets the standards of federal eligibility.

Premium cap—The premium is not to exceed 200 percent of the standard market rate.

Waiting Period for Pre-Existing Conditions and Waiver of Waiting Period:

- *Waiting period*—Coverage is excluded during a 12-month period following the effective date of coverage for a condition for which medical advice, care, diagnosis or treatment was recommended or received during the six months immediately preceding enrollment.

- *Waiver of waiting period*—The pre-existing condition limitation does not apply if the individual was continuously covered for a period of 12 months under other health insurance that was in effect up to a date that was not more than 90 days before the participant's effective date of coverage through the state health insurance pool. An individual who is federally eligible is not subject to a waiting period.

Coverage:

Wyoming offers two plans—the Brown Plan and the Gold Plan. Both plans cover the same services and differ as to the amount of deductible required and co-insurance for a specific service.

The benefits provided in the plans include:

- Inpatient hospital expense—The Brown Plan is subject to a $500 deductible per admittance. Once the deductible has been met, the insurer pays 80 percent of reasonable and customary (R&C) expenses until the out-of-pocket maximum is reached. Thereafter, 100 percent of R&C charges are covered. The Gold Plan is subject to a $250 deductible per admittance. Once the deductible has been met, the insurer pays 80 percent of R&C expenses until the out-of-pocket maximum is reached. Thereafter, 100 percent of R&C charges are covered.

- Physician services (includes inpatient and outpatient surgery)—Neither plan imposes a deductible and 80 percent of R&C charges are paid until the out-of-pocket maximum is met. Thereafter, 100 percent of R&C expenses are covered.

- Ambulance—Neither plan imposes a deductible; 80 percent of R&C charges are paid until the out-of-pocket maximum is met. Thereafter, 100 percent of R&C expenses are covered, subject to contract maximums.

- Other covered services (includes prescription drug coverage, durable medical equipment, physical therapy [20 visits per calendar year], and physician office calls). The Brown Plan is subject to a $2,000 annual deductible per individual. Once the deductible has been met, the insurer pays 70 percent of R&C expenses until the out-of-pocket maximum is reached. Thereafter, 100 percent of R&C charges are covered. The Gold Plan is subject to a $1,000 annual deductible per individual. Once the deductible has been met, the insurer pays 70 percent of R&C expenses until the out-of-pocket maximum is reached. Thereafter, 100 percent of R&C charges are covered.

- Out-of-pocket maximum—$4,000 for the Brown Plan and $2,000 for the Gold Plan.

APPENDIX 1

INSURANCE DIRECTORY

State Telephone Numbers for Health and Long-Term Care Insurance (2002)

■ ALABAMA

- **Department of Insurance**, 201 Monroe Street, Suite 1700, Montgomery, AL 36130-3351—334-241-4141
- **Alabama Health Insurance Plan** (high-risk insurance), State Employees Insurance Board, 201 Monroe Street, P.O. Box 304900, Montgomery, AL 36130-4900—877-619-2447
- **Medicaid**, 501 Dexter Avenue, Montgomery, AL 36103—334-242-5010
- **State Health Insurance Assistance Program or SHIAP** (A source for health insurance questions including Medicaid, Medigap, Medicare HMOs, individual and group plans, COBRA, consumer complaints against insurance companies, and long-term care coverage.) 770 Washington Avenue, Suite 470, Montgomery, AL 36130—800-243-5463 (in-state calls only) or 334-242-5743

■ ALASKA

- **Division of Insurance—Consumer Services Office**, 550 W. 7th Street, 15th Floor, Anchorage, AK 99503-5925—800-467-8725 (in-state calls only) or 907-269-7900
- **Medicaid, Division of Medical Assistance**, P.O. Box 110660, Juneau, AK 99811-0660—800-211-7470 (in-state calls only) or 907-465-3355

- **Alaska Comprehensive Health Insurance** (high-risk insurance), Alaska Division of Insurance, 550 W. 7th Street, 15th Floor, Anchorage, AK 99503-5925—800-467-8725 (in-state calls only) or 907-269-7900
- **Alaska Medicare Information**, Division of Senior Services (A source for health insurance questions including Medicaid, Medigap, Medicare HMOs, individual and group plans, COBRA, consumer complaints against insurance companies, and individual long-term care insurance.) 3601 C Street, Suite 310, Anchorage, AK 99503-5209—800-478-6065 (in-state calls only) or 907-269-3680

■ ARIZONA

- **Department of Insurance—Consumer Service Division**, 2910 N. 44th Street, Suite 210, Phoenix, AZ 85018—602-912-8400
- **Medicaid**, 801 E. Jefferson Street, Phoenix, AZ 85034-2246—800-654-8713(in-state calls only) or 602-417-4680
- **Benefits Assistance Department** (A source for health insurance questions including Medicaid, Medigap, Medicare HMOs, individual and group plans, COBRA, consumer complaints against insurance companies, and individual long-term care insurance.) 1366 E. Thomas Road, Suite 108, Phoenix, AZ 85014—888-763-6500 or 602-264-2255

■ ARKANSAS

- **Department of Insurance—Consumer Services Division**, 1200 W. Third Street, Little Rock, AR 72201—501-371-2649
- **Medicaid, Arkansas Department of Human Services**, Donoghey Plaza, Seventh and Main Street, P.O. Box 1347, Little Rock, AR 72203—501-682-1001
- **Comprehensive Health Insurance Plan** (high-risk insurance), Arkansas Insurance Department, 1200 W. Third Street, Little Rock, AR 72201—501-378-2523 or 800-238-8379
- **State Health Insurance Information Program or SHIIP** (A source for health insurance questions including Medicaid, Medigap, Medicare HMOs, individual and group plans, COBRA, consumer complaints against insurance companies, and individual long-term care coverage.) Arkansas Insurance Department, 1200 W. Third Street, Little Rock, AR 72201-1904—800-224-6330 or 501-371-2782

■ CALIFORNIA

- **State of California Department of Managed Health Care**, California HMO Help Center, 980 Ninth Street, Suite 500, Sacramento, CA 95814-8725—800-400-0815
- **State of California Department of Insurance**, Consumer Communications Bureau (non-HMO health insurance matters), 300 South Spring Street, South Tower, Los Angeles, CA 90013—213-897-8921
- **Medi-Cal**, 133 W. Santa Clara Street, Ventura, CA 93001—805-648-9590
- **Managed Risk Medical Insurance Program** (high-risk insurance coverage), Managed Risk Insurance Board, P.O. Box 2769, Sacramento, CA 95812-2769—916-324-4695
- **Health Insurance Counseling and Advocacy Program (HICAP)** (A source for health insurance questions including Medicaid, Medigap, Medicare HMOs, individual and group plans, COBRA, consumer complaints against insurance companies, and long-term coverage.) 1971 East 4th Street, Santa Ana, CA 92705—800-434-0222 or 714-560-0424

■ COLORADO

- **Department of Regulatory Agencies, Colorado Division of Insurance,** 1560 Broadway, Suite 850, Denver, CO 80202—800-930-3745 or 303-894-7499
- **Colorado Uninsurable Health Insurance Plan**, CUHIP, 425 S. Cherry Street, Suite 160, Denver, CO 80203—303-863-1960
- **Medicaid, Colorado Department of Health Care Policy and Financing,** 1575 Sherman Street, 10th Floor, Denver, CO 80203—303-866-6092
- **State Health Insurance Information Program or SHIIP** (A source for health insurance questions including Medicaid, Medigap, Medicare HMOs, individual and group plans, COBRA, consumer complaints against insurance companies, and long-term care insurance.) Colorado Division of Insurance, 1560 Broadway, Suite 850, Denver, CO 80202—800-544-9181 (in-state calls only) or 303-894-7499 (ext. 356)

■ CONNECTICUT

- **Department of Insurance**, P.O. Box 816, Hartford, CT 06142—860-297-3610
- **Medicaid, Division of Social Services**, 25 Sigourney Street, Hartford, CT 06106—860-424-5250

- **Connecticut Health Reinsurance Association** (high-risk insurance), c/o United Healthcare, 450 Columbus Blvd., 9NB, P.O. Box 150450, Hartford, CT 06115-0450—800-842-0004
- **State Health Insurance Information Program or SHIIP** (A source for health insurance questions including Medicaid, Medigap, Medicare HMOs, individual and group plans, COBRA, consumer complaints against insurance companies, and long-term care insurance.) Division of Elderly Services, 25 Sigourney Street, Hartford, CT 06106 —800-994-9422 (in-state calls only) or 860-424-5245

■ DELAWARE

- **Department of Insurance,** 814 Silver Lake Blvd., Rodney Bldg., Dover, DE 19904—800-282-8611 (instate calls only) or 302-739-4251
- **Medicaid—Division of Social Services**, 1901 N. Dupont Hwy, New Castle, DE 19720—800-572-2022 (in-state calls only) or 302-577-4900
- **State Health Insurance Assistance Program or SHIAP** (A source for health insurance questions including Medicaid, Medigap, Medicare HMOs, individual and group plans, COBRA, consumer complaints against insurance companies, and long-term coverage.) 841 Silver Lake Blvd., Dover, DE 19904—800-336-9500 (in-state calls only) or 302-739-6266

■ DISTRICT OF COLUMBIA

- **Insurance Administration**, 810 First Street NE, Suite 701, Washington, DC 20002—202-727-8000
- **Medicaid,** Department of Medical Assistance, 2100 Martin Luther King, Jr. Avenue NW, Washington, DC 20020-5719—202-645-4614
- **Health Insurance Counseling Project or HICP** (A source for health insurance questions including Medicaid, Medigap, Medicare HMOs, individual and group plans, COBRA, consumer complaints against insurance companies, and individual long-term care insurance. HICP is connected with the Insurance Administration.) 2136 Pennsylvania Avenue NW, First Floor, Washington, DC 20052—202-676-3900

■ FLORIDA

- **Department of Insurance**, 200 E. Gaines Street, Tallahassee, FL 32399-0300—800-342-2762 (in-state calls only) or 850-413-3100

- **Bureau of Medicaid**, 2727 Fort Knox Blvd., Tallahassee, FL 32308—850-488-3560 (The telephone number you will be dialing is to the State's Directors Office for the Bureau of Medicaid. Personnel from this office will provide telephone numbers and addresses to county offices.)
- **Florida Comprehensive Health Association** (high-risk insurance), 1210 E. Park Avenue, Tallahassee, FL 32301—850-309-1200 (Note that the office is not processing new applications. Only those individuals currently insured under the program may have their coverage renewed.)
- **Servicing Health Insurance Needs for Elders or SHINE** (A source for health insurance questions including Medicaid, Medigap, Medicare HMOs, individual and group plans, COBRA, consumer complaints against insurance companies, and long-term care coverage.) Department of Elder Affairs, 4040 Esplanada Way, Tallahassee, FL 32399-7000—800-963-5337 or 850-414-2060

GEORGIA

- **Department of Insurance**, West Tower, Suite 716, 2 Martin Luther King Drive, Atlanta, GA 30344—800-656-2298 (in-state calls only) or 404-656-2070
- **Medicaid**, 2 Peachtree NW, Floor 39, Atlanta, GA 30303—800-282-4536 (in-state calls only) or 404-656-4507
- **Health Insurance Counseling Assistance and Referral for the Elderly or HICARE** (A source for health insurance questions including Medicaid, Medigap, Medicare HMOs, individual and group plans, COBRA, consumer complaints against insurance companies, and individual long-term care coverage.) 2 Peachtree NW, Suite 36-385, Atlanta, GA 30303—800-669-8387 (in-state calls only) or 404-657-5334. For calls pertaining to clients residing in the Counties of Cherokee, Clayton, Cobb, DeKalb, Douglas, Fayette, Fulton, Gwinnette, Henry, and Rockdale, you need to telephone 404-463-3350

HAWAII

- **Commerce and Consumer Affairs, Department of Insurance Division**, 250 S. King Street, 5th Floor, Honolulu, HI 96813-4905—808-586-2790
- **Medicaid—Department of Human Services,** c/o Ms. Aileen Hiramatsu, Administrator, P.O. Box 339, Honolulu, HI 96809-0339—808-586-4997
- **Executive Office on Aging** (A source for health insurance questions including Medicaid, Medigap, Medicare HMOs, individual and group plans, COBRA, consumer complaints against insurance companies, and individual long-term

care insurance.) 250 S. Hotel Street, Suite 406, Honolulu, HI 96813-2831—808-586-7299 or 888-825-9229

■ IDAHO

- **Department of Insurance**, Consumer Assistance Office, 700 W. State Street, Third Floor, Boise, ID 83720-0043—208-334-4342
- **Medicaid, Idaho Department of Health and Welfare**, 3380 Americana Terrace, Boise, ID 83720—208-334-5747
- **State Health Insurance Assistance Program a/k/a Senior Health Insurance Benefits Advisers or SHIBA** (A source on health insurance questions including Medicaid, Medicare HMOs, individual and group plans, COBRA, consumer complaints against insurance companies, and individual long-term coverage. SHIBA is a division of the Idaho Dept. of Insurance.) 700 W. State Street, Third Floor, Boise, ID 83720-0043—800-247-4422 (in-state calls only) or 208-334-4250.

■ ILLINOIS

- **Department of Insurance (Springfield Office)**, 320 W. Washington Street, Springfield, IL 62767—217-782-4515 or (Chicago Office), 100 W. Randolph, Suite 15–100, Chicago, IL 60601—312-814-2420
- **Medicaid, Department of Public Aid**, 201 S. Grand Avenue, Springfield, IL 62763—800-252-8635
- **Illinois Comprehensive Health Insurance** (high-risk insurance), 400 W. Monroe Street, Suite 202, Springfield, IL 62704—217-558-6202
- **Office of Consumer Health Insurance** (Established on January 1, 2000, the office will answer questions on health insurance including explaining provisions contained in a specific health plan, the legal rights guaranteed a health care consumer, and assistance on a complaint against an insurer.) 320 W. Washington Street, Springfield, IL 62767—877-527-9431 (in-state calls only) or 217-782-4515
- **Senior Health Insurance Program or SHIP** (A source for health insurance questions including Medicaid, Medigap, Medicare HMOs, individual and group plans, COBRA, consumer complaints against insurance companies, and individual long-term care coverage.) 320 W. Washington Street, Springfield, IL 62767-0001—800-548-9034 (in-state calls only) or 217-524-1631

■ INDIANA

- **Department of Insurance**, 311 W. Washington Street, Suite 300, Indianapolis, IN 46204—800-622-4461 (in-state calls only) or 317-232-2395
- **Electronic Data Systems** (Information on State of Indiana Medicaid)—800-577-1278 or 317-488-5018
- **Indiana Comprehensive Health Insurance Association** (high-risk insurance) Outsourced Administrative Systems, Inc., 4550 Victory Lane, Indianapolis, IN 46203—800-552-7921 or 317-614-2000/317-297-6800
- **Senior Health Insurance Information Program or SHIIP** (A source for health insurance questions including Medicaid, Medigap, Medicare HMOs, individual and group plans, COBRA, consumer complaints against insurance companies, and individual long-term care coverage.) 311 W. Washington Street, Suite 300, Indianapolis, IN 46204—800-452-4800 (in-state calls only) or 317-233-3475

■ IOWA

- **Division of Insurance**, Health Insurance, 330 Maple Street, Des Moines, IA 50319—877-955-1212 (in-state calls only) or 515-281-6348
- **Medicaid, Division of Medical Services**, Hoover State Office Bldg., Fifth Floor, Des Moines, IA 50319—800-972-2017
- **Division of Insurance**, Iowa Consumer Affairs Bureau, 330 Maple Street, Des Moines, IA 50319—515-281-4241 (This bureau handles consumer complaints and questions from the public. The unit conducts investigations and, when necessary, brings actions against insurance companies.)
- **Iowa Comprehensive Health Association (ICHA)** (high-risk insurance), P.O. Box 33728, Indianapolis, IN 46203-0728—800-877-5156
- **Senior Health Insurance Information Program or SHIIP** (A source for health insurance questions including Medicaid, Medigap, Medicare HMOs, individual and group plans, COBRA, consumer complaints against insurance companies, and individual long-term care coverage.) 330 Maple Street, Des Moines, IA 50319—800-351-4664 or 515-281-6867)

■ KANSAS

- **Department of Insurance**, Consumer Insurance Affairs Bureau, 420 S.W. Ninth Street, Topeka, KS 66612-1678—800-432-2484 (in-state calls only) or 785-296-2348

- **Medicaid**, 915 S.W. Harrison Street, D.S.O.B., Room 652, Topeka, KS 66612—785-296-3981
- **Kansas Health Insurance Association** (high-risk insurance), P.O. Box 1090, Great Bend, KS 67530—800-290-1368
- **Senior Health Insurance Counseling for Kansas or SHICK** (A source for health insurance questions including Medicaid, Medigap, Medicare HMOs, individual and group plans, COBRA, consumer complaints against insurance companies, and long-term care coverage.) 130 S. Market Street, Suite 1028, P.O. Box 3850, Wichita, KS 67201-3850—800-860-5260 (in-state calls only) or 316-337-7386

■ KENTUCKY

- **Department of Insurance**, 215 W. Main Street, P.O. Box 517, Frankfort, KY 40602—502-564-6027 or 800-595-6053
- **Medicaid, Department of Health Services**, 275 E. Main Street, Frankfort, KY 40621—502-564-4321
- **Division of Consumer Protection and Education** (A division assisting consumers in complaints against insurance companies.) P.O. Box 517, Frankfort, KY 40602—800-595-6053 (in-state calls only) or 502-564-6034
- **Kentucky Access** (high-risk insurance), P.O. Box 33707, Indianapolis, IN 46203-0707—866-405-6145
- **Benefits Counseling Section of the Office of Aging** (A source for health insurance questions including Medicaid, Medigap, Medicare HMOs, individual and group plans, COBRA, consumer complaints against insurance companies, and long-term care coverage.) 275 E. Main Street, Frankfort, KY 40621—877-293-7447 (in-state calls only) or 502-564-6930

■ LOUISIANA

- **Department of Insurance**, P.O. Box 94214, 950 N. Fifth Street, Baton Rouge, LA 70804—800-259-5300 (in-state calls only) or 225-342-5900
- **Medicaid, Department of Health and Hospital Services**, 1201 Capital Access, Baton Rouge, LA 70802; P.O. Box 91030, Baton Rouge, LA 70821-9030—225-342-3891
- **Louisiana Health Plan** (high-risk insurance), P.O. Drawer 83880, Baton Rouge, LA 70884-3880—800-736-0947 or 225-926-6245

- **Senior Health Insurance Information Program (SHIIP)** (A source for health insurance questions including Medicaid, Medigap, Medicare HMOs, individual and group plans, COBRA, and long-term care insurance.) 950 N. Fifth Street, Baton Rouge, LA 70804—800-259-5300 (in-state calls only) or 225-342-5900

■ MAINE

- **Bureau of Insurance**, 35 State House Station, Augusta, ME 04333—800-300-5000 (in-state calls only) or 207-624-8475
- **Medicaid, Bureau of Medical Services**, 11 State House Station, Augusta, ME 04335-0011—800-321-5557 (in-state calls only) or 207-287-2546
- **Bureau of Elder or Adult Services** (A source for health insurance questions including Medicaid, Medigap, Medicare HMOs, individual and group plans, COBRA, and long-term care insurance.) 35 Anthony Lane, Augusta, ME 04333—800-262-2232 (in-state calls only) or 207-624-5335

■ MARYLAND

- **Insurance Administration**, Life and Health Division, 525 Street Paul Place, Baltimore, MD 21202—800-492-6116 or 410-468-2000
- **Department of Long-Term Care Services** (A source to obtain information on nursing home, home health, and adult daycare services), 201 W. Preston Street, Baltimore, MD 21201—877-633-4664 (in-state calls only) or 410-767-1444
- **Medicaid, Recipient Relations Unit**, 201 W. Preston Street, Room L-9, Baltimore, MD 21201—800-492-5231 (in-state calls only) or 410-767-5800
- **Maryland Department of Aging** (A source for health insurance questions including Medicaid, Medigap, Medicare HMOs, individual and group plans, COBRA, and long-term care insurance), 301 W. Preston Street, Suite 1007, Baltimore, MD 21204—800-423-3425 (in-state calls only), 410-767-1100, or TTY: 410-767-1083

■ MASSACHUSETTS

- **Division of Insurance—Consumer Health Line**, 1 South Station, Boston, MA 02110—617-521-7794
- **Medicaid—Customer Service, Division of Medical Assistance**, 55 Summer Street, Boston, MA 02112—800-841-2900

- **MassHealth** (A comprehensive health insurance and premium assistance program for senior citizens and disabled individuals), 300 Ocean Avenue, Revere, MA 02151—800-841-2900
- **Senior Health Insurance Needs for Elders or SHINE** (A source for health insurance questions including Medicaid, Medigap, Medicare HMOs, individual and group plans, COBRA, complaints against insurance companies, and long-term care insurance coverage.) 1 Ashburton Place, Boston, MA 02108—800-882-2003 (in-state calls only), 617-222-7441 or TTY: 800-872-0166

■ MICHIGAN

- **Department of Commerce, Division of Insurance**, P.O. Box 30220, Lansing, MI 48909—517-373-0220 or 877-999-6442
- **Medicaid—Family Independence Agency**, P.O. Box 30037, Lansing, MI 48909—517-373-3035
- **Michigan Medicare Medicaid Assistance Program** (A source for health insurance questions including Medicaid, Medigap, Medicare HMOs, individual and group plans, COBRA, complaints against insurance companies, and long-term care insurance coverage.) 6105 W. Street Joseph Hwy., Suite 209, Lansing, MI 48917-4850—800-803-7174 or 517-886-0899

■ MINNESOTA

- **Department of Commerce—Insurance Enforcement Division** (The Insurance Enforcement Division regulates health insurance except in matters involving HMOs.) 85 Seventh Place East, St. Paul, MN 55101—800-657-3602 or 651-296-2488
- **Department of Health** (Regulates matters pertaining to HMOs.), 121 E. Seventh Place, Metro Square Building, Suite 400, St. Paul, MN 55101-2117—800-657-3916 (in-state calls only) or 651-282-5608
- **Medicaid, Department of Human Services**, 444 Lafayette Rd., St. Paul, MN 55101—800-657-3739
- **Minnesota Comprehensive Health Association** (high-risk insurance), 5775 Wayzata Blvd., St. Louis Park, MN 55416—952-593-9609
- **Minnesota Board of Aging** (A source for health insurance questions including Medicaid, Medigap, Medicare HMOs, individual and group plans, COBRA, complaints against insurance companies, and long-term care insurance coverage.) 444 Lafayette Rd., St. Paul, MN 55164—651-296-2770 or 800-882-6262

■ MISSISSIPPI

- **Insurance Department—Consumer Services Division** (Telephone numbers for general insurance information and filing a complaint against an insurance company.), 501 Northwest Street, Suite 1001 Woolfolk State Office Bldg., Jackson, MS 39201—800-562-2957 (in-state calls only) or 601-359-2453

- **Medicaid Division**, 239 N. Lamar Street, Jackson, MS 39201—800-421-2408 (in-state calls only) or 601-359-6050

- **Mississippi Comprehensive Health Insurance Risk Pool Association** (high-risk insurance), Risk Pool Association, P.O. Box 13748, Jackson, MS 39236—601-362-0799 or 888-820-9400

- **Mississippi Insurance and Counseling Program or MICAP** (A source for health insurance questions including Medicaid, Medigap, Medicare HMOs, individual and group plans, COBRA, complaints against insurance companies, and long-term care coverage.) 750 N. State Street, Jackson, MS 39202—800-948-3090 or 601-359-4929

■ MISSOURI

- **Department of Insurance—Consumer Affairs Division**, 301 W. High Street, Jefferson City, MO 39205/P.O. Box 79, Jefferson City, MO 65101—800-726-7390 or 573-751-4126

- **Medicaid—Division of Medical Services**, 615 Howerton Court, Jefferson City, MO 65109—573-751-3425

- **Missouri Health Insurance Pool** (high-risk insurance) 1831 Chestnut Street, St. Louis, MO 63103—314-923-4444 (For individuals residing in Kansas City, MO, or adjacent counties, the address to contact is P.O. Box 8966, Kansas City, MO 64114 and the telephone number is 800-821-2231.)

- **Missouri CLAIMS (Community Leaders Assisting the Insured of Missouri) Program** (A source for health insurance questions including Medicaid, Medigap, Medicare HMOs, individual and group plans, COBRA, complaints against insurance companies, and long-term care insurance coverage.) 3425 Constitution Court E., Jefferson City, MO 65109—800-390-3330

■ MONTANA

- **State Auditor's Office, Insurance Division** (issues relating to health insurance) 840 Helena Avenue, Helena, MT 59601—800-332-6148 (in-state calls only) or 406-444-2040

- **Medicaid c/o ACS**, 37 N. Last Chance Gulch, Helena, MT 59601-4164—800-624-8958 (in-state calls only) or 406-442-1837
- **Montana Comprehensive Health Association** (high-risk insurance) c/o Blue Cross and Blue Shield of Montana, P.O. Box 4309, 560 N. Park Avenue, Helena, MT 59604—406-444-8537
- **State Health Insurance Assistance Program or SHIP** (A source for health insurance questions including Medicaid, Medigap, Medicare HMOs, individual and group plans, COBRA, complaints against insurance companies, and long-term care insurance coverage.) 111 Sanders, Helena, MT 59620—800-332-2272 (in-state calls only) or 406-444-7781

■ NEBRASKA

- **Department of Insurance—Life and Health Division**, 941 O Street, Suite 400, Lincoln, NE 68508—800-234-7119 or 402-471-2201
- **Medicaid—Department of Health and Human Services**, P.O. Box 95026, Lincoln, NE 68509—800-430-3244 or 402-471-9147
- **Nebraska Comprehensive Health Insurance Pool** (high-risk insurance), Blue Cross and Blue Shield of Nebraska, P.O. Box 3248, Main Post Office, Omaha, NE 68180-0001—402-343-3337
- **Nebraska Health Insurance Information, Counseling and Assistance Program or NICA** (A source for health insurance questions including Medicaid, Medigap, Medicare HMOs, individual and group plans, COBRA, complaints against insurance companies, and long-term care insurance coverage.) 941 O Street, Lincoln, NE 68508—800-234-7119 or 402-471-2201

■ NEVADA

- **Department of Business and Industry—Division of Insurance**, 788 Fairview Drive, Suite 300, Carson City, NV 89701-5491—775-687-4270
- **Medicaid—Nevada Department of Human Resources—Division of Health Care Financing and Policy**, 1350 E. Ninth Street, Reno, NV 89512—775-448-5000
- **State Health Insurance Assistance Program or SHIP—Division of Aging Services** (A source for health insurance questions including Medicaid, Medigap, Medicare HMOs, individual and group plans, COBRA, complaints against insurance companies, and long-term care insurance coverage.) West Sahara Street, Las Vegas, NV 89102—800-307-4444 or 702-486-3478

■ NEW HAMPSHIRE

- **Department of Insurance—Consumer Division**, 56 Old Suncook Road, Concord, NH 03301-7317—800-852-3416 or 603-271-2261
- **Medicaid Client Services—Consumer Assistance Office**—6 Hazen Drive, Concord, NH 03301—800-852-3345 ext. 4344 (in-state calls only) or 603-271-4501
- **Health Insurance Counseling Education Assistance Services or HICEAS** (A source for health insurance questions including Medicaid, Medigap, Medicare HMOs, individual and group plans, individual prescription drug assistance program, COBRA, complaints against insurance companies, and long-term care insurance coverage.) P.O. Box 2338, Concord, NH 03302-2338—800-852-3388 (in-state calls only) or 603-225-9000

■ NEW JERSEY

- **Department of Banking and Insurance—Life and Health Section**, P.O. Box 325, Trenton, NJ 08640-0325—609-292-5427
- **Medicaid—Division of Medical Assistance and Health Services**, P.O. Box 712, Trenton NJ 08625-0712—609-588-2600
- **Pharmaceutical Assistance to the Aged and Disabled OR PAAD**, P.O. Box 715, Trenton, NJ 08625—800-792-9745 (in-state calls only)
- **Department of Banking and Insurance—Consumer Protection**, P.O. Box 329, Trenton, NJ 08640-0329—609-292-5316
- **Department of Health and Senior Services—State Health Insurance Assistance Program or SHIP** (A source for health insurance on Medicaid, Medigap, Medicare HMOs, insurance plans, individual prescription drug assistance program (PAAD), COBRA, complaints against insurance companies, and long-term care insurance coverage.) P.O. Box 807, Trenton, NJ 08618—800-792-8820 (in-state calls only) or 609-588-3139

■ NEW MEXICO

- **New Mexico Department of Insurance—Life and Health Division**, PERA Building, Room 519, 1120 Paseo de Peralta, Santa Fe, NM 87501—800-947-4722 (in-state calls only) or 505-827-4555
- **Medicaid—Human Services Department Medical Assistance Division Help Desk**, P.O. Box 2348, Santa Fe, NM 87504-2348—888-997-2583 (in-state calls only) or 505-827-3100

- **New Mexico Comprehensive Health Insurance Pool**, P.O. Box 27630, Albuquerque, NM 87125-7630—800-432-0750
- **State Agency for Aging** (A source for health insurance questions including Medicaid, Medigap, Medicare HMOs, individual and group plans, individual prescription drug assistance program, COBRA, complaints against insurance companies, and long-term care insurance coverage.) 228 E. Palace Avenue, Santa Fe, NM 87501—800-432-2080 (in-state calls only) or 505-827-7640

■ NEW YORK

- **Department of Insurance**—The following are regional addresses and telephone numbers that may be used for consumer complaints against insurance companies and inquiries on health insurance:
  - **New York City**—5 Beaver Street, NY 10004—212-480-6400
  - **Albany**—1 Empire State Plaza, Albany, NY 12257—866-432-5849
  - **Buffalo**—65 Court Street, Buffalo, NY 14202—716- 847-7618
  - **Minneola**—200 Old Country Road, Suite 340, Minneola, NY 11501—516-248-5886
- **Medicaid Help line**, 99 Washington Avenue, Albany, NY 12210—518-486-9057
- **New York State Office of the Aging** (A source for health insurance questions including Medicaid, Medigap, Medicare HMOs, individual and group plans, individual prescription drug assistance program, COBRA, complaints against insurance companies, and long-term care insurance coverage.) 112 State Street, Room 710, Albany, NY 12207—518-447-7177 and Medicare Rights Center—212-869-3850 or outside New York City 800-333-4114

■ NORTH CAROLINA

- **Department of Insurance**, P.O. Box 26387, 430 N. Salisbury Street, Raleigh, NC 27611—800-546-5664 (in-state calls only) or 919-733-7349
- **Medicaid Assistance—Department of Health and Human Services**, 2512 Mail Service Center, Raleigh, NC 27698-2512—919-857-4019
- **Senior Health Insurance Information Program or SHIIP** (A source for health insurance questions including Medicaid, Medigap, Medicare HMOs, individual and group plans, COBRA, complaints against insurance companies, and long-term care insurance coverage.) 111 Seaboard Avenue, Raleigh, NC 27604—800-443-9354 (in-state calls only) or 919-733-0111

■ NORTH DAKOTA

- **Department of Insurance—Health Insurance Hotline**, 600 E. Boulevard, 5th Floor, Bismarck, ND 58505 —800-247-0560 or 701-328-2440
- **Medicaid Assistance—Department of Human Services Medical Services Division**, 600 E. Boulevard, Dept. 325, Bismarck, ND 58505—800-755-2604 or 701-328-2321
- **Comprehensive Health Association of North Dakota or CHAND** (high-risk insurance) Blue Cross and Blue Shield of North Dakota, 4310 13th Avenue S.W., Fargo, ND 58121—800-737-0016 or 701-277-2271
- **Senior Health Insurance Counseling or SHIC** (A source for health insurance questions including Medicaid, Medigap, Medicare HMOs, individual and group plans, COBRA, complaints against insurance companies, and long-term care insurance coverage.) 600 E. Boulevard, Bismarck, ND 58505—800-247-0560 or 701-328-2440

■ OHIO

- **Department of Insurance—Managed Care Division**, 2100 Stella Court, Columbus, OH 43215—614-644-2661
- **Medicaid Division—Department of Human Services**, 30 E. Broad Street, Columbus, OH 43266—614-466-0140
- **Department of Insurance—Consumer Hotline**, 2100 Stella Court, Columbus, OH 43215—800-686-1526 (office to file complaints)
- **Ohio Senior Insurance Information Program or OSHIIP** (A source for health insurance questions including Medicaid, Medigap, Medicare HMOs, individual and group plans, COBRA, complaints against insurance companies, and long-term care insurance coverage.) 2100 Stella Court, Columbus, OH 43215—800-686-1578 (in-state calls only) or 614-644-3458

■ OKLAHOMA

- **Department of Insurance—Life and Health Division**, 2401 N.W. 23rd Street, Suite 28, Oklahoma City, OK 73107/P.O. Box 53408, Oklahoma City, OK 73152—800-522-0071 (in-state calls only) or 405-521-3541
- **Medicaid—Department of Social Services**, 2409 N. Kelly Avenue, Oklahoma City, OK 73111-2698—405-522-5818

- **Oklahoma Health Insurance High Risk Pool**, P.O. Box 50429, Midwest City, OK 73140-5429—405-741-8434
- **Senior Health Insurance Counseling Program or SHICP** (A source for health insurance questions including Medicaid, Medigap, Medicare HMOs, individual and group plans, COBRA, complaints against insurance companies, and long-term care insurance coverage.) 2401 N.W. 23rd Street, Suite 28, Oklahoma City, OK 73107—800-763-2828 (in-state calls only) or 405-521-6628

■ OREGON

- **Department of Consumer and Business Services—Life and Health Insurance Division**, 350 Winters Street NE, Room 440, Salem, OR 97301-3883—800-722-4134 (in-state calls only) or 503-947-7984
- **Oregon Health Plan—Adult and Family Service Division (Medicaid)**, P.O. Box 14520, Salem, OR 97309—800-699-9075 (in-state calls only) or 503-378-2666
- **Oregon Medical Insurance Pool** (high-risk insurance.) 250 Church Street SE, Suite 200, Salem, OR 97301-3921—503-373-1692
- **Senior Health Insurance Benefits Assistance Program or SHIBA** (A source for health insurance questions including Medicaid, Medigap, Medicare HMOs, individual and group plans, COBRA, complaints against insurance companies, premium assistance, and long-term care insurance coverage.) 350 Winters Street NE, Room 440, Salem, OR 97301-3883—800-722-4134 (in-state calls only) or 503-947-7984

■ PENNSYLVANIA

- **Department of Insurance—Consumer Information and Complaint**, 1321 Strawberry Square, Harrisburg, PA 17120—717-787-2317 (You may also contact the Consumer Information and Complaint Office at the following locations: Philadelphia—215-560-2630, Pittsburgh—412-565-5020, Erie—814-871-4466)
- **Department of Public Welfare—Medicaid Recipient Hotline**, 1401 N. Seventh Street, Harrisburg, PA 17105—800-692-7462
- **Apprise Health Care and Counseling—Department of Aging** (A source for health insurance questions including Medicaid, Medigap, Medicare HMOs, individual and group plans, COBRA, complaints against insurance companies, and long-term care insurance coverage.) 555 Walnut Street, Harrisburg, PA 17101-1919—717-783-8975

■ RHODE ISLAND

- **Department of Business Regulations Insurance Division Office of Life and Health**, 233 Richmond Street, Suite 233 Providence, RI 02903-4233—401-222-2223
- **Department of Human Services—Medicaid**, 206 Elmwood Avenue, Providence, RI 02907—401-222-7000
- **Rhode Island Department of Elderly Affairs** (A source for health insurance questions including Medicaid, Medigap, Medicare HMOs, individual and group plans, COBRA, complaints against insurance companies, and long-term care insurance coverage.) 160 Pine Street, Providence, RI 02903—401-222-2880

■ SOUTH CAROLINA

- **Department of Insurance—Life, Accident, and Health Division**, 300 Arbor Lake Drive, Suite 1200, Columbia, SC 29223—800-768-3467 (in-state calls only) or 803-737-6180
- **Department of Social Services—Medical (Medicaid) Division**—803-898-9470
- **South Carolina Health Insurance Pool** (high-risk insurance.) Blue Cross and Blue Shield of South Carolina, P.O. Box 61173, Columbia, SC 29260-1173—800-868-2500, ext. 42757 or 803-788-0500, ext. 42757
- **South Carolina Bureau of Senior Services** (A source for health insurance questions including Medicaid, Medigap, Medicare HMOs, individual and group plans, COBRA, complaints against insurance companies, and long-term care insurance coverage.) 1801 Main Street, Columbia, SC 29202-8206—800-868-9095 (in-state calls only) or 803-898-2850

■ SOUTH DAKOTA

- **Division of Insurance,** 118 W. Capitol, Pierre, SD 57501-2000—605-773-3563
- **Department of Social Services—Medicaid**, 700 Governors Drive, Pierre, SD 57501—605-773-4678
- **Adult Services and Aging** (A source for health insurance questions including Medicaid, Medigap, Medicare HMOs, individual and group plans, COBRA, complaints against insurance companies, premium payment assistance [a/k/a QMB and SLMB], and long-term care insurance coverage.) 700 Governors Drive, Pierre, SD 57501—800-822-8804 (in-state calls only) or 605-773-3656

■ TENNESSEE

- **Department of Insurance—Consumer Insurance Services Office**, 500 James Robertson Parkway, 4th Floor, Nashville, TN 37243—800-342-4029 (in-state calls only) or 615-741-2218
- **Department of Human Services—TennCare** (high-risk insurance or Medicaid), 729 Church Street, Nashville, TN 37247—Bureau of TennCare, TennCare Select, P.O. Box 22630 Nashville, TN 37202-2630—800-669-1851
- **Insurance Assistance Office for Seniors** (A source for health insurance questions including Medicaid, Medigap, Medicare HMOs, individual and group plans, COBRA, complaints against insurance companies, the Tenn-Care Program, and long-term care insurance coverage.) 500 James Robertson Parkway, 4th Floor, Nashville, TN 37243—800-525-2816 (in-state calls only) or 615-741-4955

■ TEXAS

- **Department of Insurance—Consumer Protection Division**, 333 Guadalupe, Austin, TX 78701/P.O. Box 149091, Austin, TX 78714-9091—800-252-3439 or 512-463-6515
- **Department of Human Services—Medicaid**, 701 W. 51st Street, Austin, TX 78751—800-252-8263 or 512-438-3280
- **Texas Health Insurance Risk Pool** (high-risk insurance) 2512 South IH-35 #110, Austin, TX 78704—512-441-7665
- **Texas Department on Aging (a HICAP program)** (A source for health insurance questions including Medicaid, Medigap, Medicare HMOs, individual and group plans, COBRA, complaints against insurance companies, premium assistance, and long-term care insurance coverage.) 4900 Lamar Blvd., Austin, TX 78751/P.O. Box 12786, Austin, TX 78711—800-252-9240

■ UTAH

- **Insurance Department—Consumer Service Assistance**, 310 State Office Building, Suite 3110 Salt Lake City, UT 84114—800-439-3805 (in-state calls only) or 801-538-3077
- **Insurance Department—Health Insurance Complaint Division**, 310 State Office Building, Salt Lake City, UT 85114—801-538-3805 (Salt Lake City only) or 800-350-6242 (for remaining areas of the state)
- **Utah Comprehensive Health Insurance Pool**, P.O. Box 30270, Salt Lake City, UT 84130—801-333-5573

- **Department of Health—Medicaid**—801-538-7088 or 800-662-9651
- **State Health Insurance Assistance Program or SHIP (a/k/a Aging and Adult Services)** (A source for health insurance questions including Medicaid, Medigap, Medicare HMOs, individual and group plans, COBRA, complaints against insurance companies, and long-term care insurance coverage.) 120 North 200 West, Room 325, Salt Lake City, UT 84103—800-541-7735 (in-state calls only) or 801-538-3910

■ VERMONT

- **Department of Banking, Insurance, Securities, and Health Care Administration**, 89 Main Street, Drawer 20, Montpelier, VT 05620-3101—802-828-3301
- **Vermont Division of Health Care Administration** (Information provided on health plans, health insurance and health care services available in Vermont.) Third Floor, 89 Main Street, Montpelier, VT 05620—800-631-7788 (in-state calls only) or 802-828-2900
- **Department of Health and Human Services—Medicaid** (Address will be provided at time of call)—800-250-8427
- **Prescription Drug Assistance** (There are four programs available in Vermont namely, VHAP Pharmacy, VHAP Script, and New V Script, for individuals who are under 65 years old, on Medicare, and are disabled; and VHAP Managed Care available to people who are under 65, disabled, not on Medicare, not Medicaid-eligible, but whose incomes are below a certain level.) (Address will be provided at time of call)—800-250-8427
- **Office of Health Care Ombudsman** (Separate state office providing information on patient rights and consumer complaints against health insurers.) 264 N. Winooski Avenue, Burlington, VT 05402—800-917-7787 (in-state calls only) or 802-863-2316
- **Vermont Department of Aging and Disabilities** (A source for health insurance questions including Medicaid, Medigap, Medicare HMOs, individual and group plans, COBRA, complaints against insurance companies, prescription drug assistance, and long-term care insurance coverage.) 103 S. Main Street, Waterbury, VT 05671—800-642-5119 (in-state calls only) or 802-241-2400

■ VIRGINIA

- **State Corporation Commission, Bureau of Insurance**, 1300 E. Main Street, Richmond, VA 23219—800-552-7945 (in-state calls only) or 804-371-9691

- **Department of Social Services—Medical Assistance Services (Medicaid)**, 600 E. Broad Street, Richmond VA 23 219—804-786-7933
- **Department of Aging** (A source for health insurance questions including Medicaid, Medigap, Medicare HMOs, individual and group plans, COBRA, complaints against insurance companies, and long-term care insurance coverage.) 1600 Forest Avenue, Richmond, VA 23229—800-552-3402 (in-state calls only) or 804-662-9333

■ WASHINGTON

- **State Insurance Commission—Office of Consumer Protection and Information**, P.O. Box 40256, Olympia, WA 98504-0256—800-562-6900 or 360-753-7301
- **Department of Health and Social Services—Medical Assistance Customer Service Center (Medicaid)**, 1011 Plum Street, Olympia, WA 98504-5532—800-562-3022
- **Washington State Health Insurance Pool** (high-risk insurance), c/o Mary Childress, Compliance Manager/Life and Disability, Insurance Building, P.O. Box 33727, Indianapolis, IN 46203-0727—800-877-5187
- **State Health Insurance Benefits Advisor Program or SHIBA** (A source for health insurance questions including Medicaid, Medigap, Medicare HMOs, individual and group plans, COBRA, complaints against insurance companies, and long-term care insurance coverage.)—800-397-4422

■ WEST VIRGINIA

- **Commission of Insurance—Health Insurance Consumer Division**, 1124 Smith Street, Room 309, Charleston, WV 25301—304-558-3386
- **Department of Health and Human Resources—Medicaid**, 350 Capitol Street, Charleston, WV 25303-0540—304-558-2400
- **State Health Insurance Network or SHINE (a/k/a Bureau of Senior Services)** (A source for health insurance questions including Medicaid, Medigap, Medicare HMOs, individual and group plans, COBRA, complaints against insurance companies, and long-term care insurance coverage.) Capitol Bldg., 1900 Kanawha Blvd., Charleston, WV 25305—877-987-4463 or 304-558-3317

■ WISCONSIN

- **Insurance Commission**, 121 E. Wilson Street, Madison, WI 53702/P.O. Box 7873, Madison, WI 53707-7873—608-266-3585
- **Medicaid and Badger Care Services**, P.O. Box 6678, Madison, WI 53716—800-362-3002
- **Wisconsin Health Insurance Risk Sharing Plan or HIRSP** (high-risk insurance), Wisconsin Health Insurance Risk Sharing Plan, 6406 Bridge Road, Suite 18, Madison, WI 53784—800-828-4777
- **Area Agency on Aging** (A source for health insurance questions including Medicaid, Medigap, Medicare HMOs, individual and group plans, county-based prescription drug programs, COBRA, insurance complaints, and long-term care insurance coverage.) 125 N. Executive Drive, Suite 102, Brookfield, WI 53005—877-333-0202 or 262-821-4444

■ WYOMING

- **Department of Insurance** (consumer information or complaints), 122 W. 25th Street, Herschler Bldg., Third Floor East, Cheyenne, WY 82002—800-438-5768 (in-state calls only) or 307-777-7401/7402
- **Department of Health—Medicaid Division**, 6101 Yellowstone Road, Cheyenne, WY 82002—800-252-1269 (in-state calls only) or 307-777-5520
- **Wyoming Health Insurance Pool** (high-risk insurance) 4000 House Avenue, Cheyenne, WY 82009—800-442-2376 (in-state calls only) or 307-634-1393
- **Wyoming Senior Citizen Program** (A source for health insurance questions including Medicaid, Medigap, Medicare HMOs, individual and group plans, COBRA, complaints against insurance companies, and long-term care insurance coverage.) P.O. Box B D, Riverton, WY 82501—800-856-4398 (in-state calls only) or 307-856-6880

APPENDIX 2

USEFUL WEB SITES

- **Agency for Healthcare Research and Quality—www.ahcpr.gov**—Provides information in the areas of managed care, mental health, long-term care, and governmental resources.
- **Center for Medicare and Medicaid Services—www.cms.gov**—Provides information about Medicare, Medicaid, and the State Children's Health Insurance Program (SCHIP).
- **Center for Medicare Advocacy—www.medicareadvocacy.org**—Nonprofit organization providing legal advice, self-help materials, and representation for elders and people with disabilities who are unfairly denied Medicare coverage.
- **Dictionary.com—www.dictionary.com**—Online dictionary and thesaurus.
- **Duke Center for Health Policy, Law and Management—www.hpolicy.duke.edu**—Provides an extensive list of health care links including:
  - Federal legislative information on the Thomas web site;
  - Code of federal regulations;
  - Robert Wood Johnson web site; and
  - Regional foundations
- **Families USA—www.familiesusa.org**—Provides links to documents pertaining to a variety of health care reform issues including managed care, assistance to the uninsured, and key state bills and legislation.
- **Free and low cost prescription drugs**—A listing of drugs whose manufacturers have patient assistance programs:
  - www.institute-dc.org or
  - www.needymeds.com or

- **www.themedicineprogram.com**—Web site for the Medicine Program, an operation that processes applications for patients who cannot afford their prescriptions.
- **Georgetown University Medical Center Health Care Research and Policy Web site www.healthinsuranceinfo.net**—Examines the legal protections provided by each state regarding an individual's procurement of group or individual health coverage.
- **Google Search Engine**—<www.google.com/search?q=Health+Insurance+Portability+and+Accountability+Act>—Site provides numerous links to the HIPAA statute.
- **GovSpot—www.govspot.com**—Provides information to online government services including access to public search engines and frequently requested federal 800 numbers.
- **Health Finder—www.health-connect.com**—Health Finder is a search tool providing health care resources on the Internet. Search directories include sites for:
  - Home health care;
  - Long-term care;
  - Health associations; and
  - Financial and insurance assistance.
- **Health Hippo—http://hippo.findlaw.com**—Hippo is an extensive health information site examining issues ranging from health insurance bills being considered by Congress to the Medicare + Choice program and the Patient Bill of Rights. Health Hippo also includes an array of search engines providing well over 100 links to other health care sites.
- **Health Insurance Association of America (HIAA)—www.hiaa.org**—The HIAA is a trade association for companies in the private health care system. Site contains guides on managed care, health insurance, and long-term care, and includes an insurance counseling directory.
- **Health Insurance Glossary—www.insweb.com/research/merritt/health%2Da.htm**—Definition of terms commonly used when discussing health insurance matters.
- **Independent Living Centers—www.ilusa.com/links/ilcenters.htm#AR**—National listing of independent living centers.
- **Insure.Com—www.insure.com/health**—Site provides information on the following subjects:
  - COBRA;
  - HIPAA;
  - Individual Health Insurance; and

- Effect of divorce on one's health insurance.
- **Managed Health Care Glossary**—www.pohly.com/terms.html—Provides definitions of terms commonly used by physicians, hospitals, and managed care providers.
- **Medicare—The Official U.S. Government Site for Medicare Information**—www.medicare.gov—Contains extensive information on Medicare including access to related Web sites. Site also provides telephone numbers nationwide to offices familiar with insurers selling Medicare Supplement and Medigap coverage, the state's open enrollment policy, and questions pertaining to COBRA, HIPAA, and Medicaid.

    The site also provides information on how to apply for drug assistance through drug companies, states, community-based programs, and disease-specific programs. Users can enter their ZIP codes to search what benefits are offered in their communities.

    Another useful feature is located on the Nursing Home Compare page. Users will now be able to obtain and compare information from Center for Medicare and Medicaid Services' (formerly the Health Care Financing Administration) last three surveys of each of the 16,500 nursing homes participating in Medicare and Medicaid. Previously, only the most current survey was available through the site.
- **Medicare Rights Center**—www.medicarerights.org—Web site offers information to consumers and professionals on Medicare including counseling by e-mail.
- **National Aging Administration Center**—www.aoa.gov/naic/Notes/—(Upon accessing site, scroll down and select "prescription drugs.") Site provides extensive information on prescriptive drugs including:
    - Internet pharmacies;
    - Purchasing medical products online;
    - Drug interaction information;
    - Disclosure of wholesale cost of prescriptive drugs; and
    - State prescription drug assistance programs.
- **National Association of Insurance Commissioners**—www.naic.org—The NAIC is the national organization of state insurance commissioners and its site concentrates on current state health insurance regulations and policy.
- **National Health Law Program**—www.healthlaw.org—Includes an overview of Medicaid, a fact sheet on the prescription drug programs, and links to state Medicaid sites on the Internet.
- **National Library of Medicine**—www.nlm.nih.gov—Site provides access to a number of health organizations, abstracts from over 4,300 biomedical journals, and extensive consumer health information.

- **National Organization of Social Security Claimants' Representatives (NOSSCR)**—www.nosscr.org—National organization of attorneys specializing in Social Security matters including Social Security Disability Insurance and supplemental security income. Links to numerous government sites.
- **Pharmaceutical Research and Manufacturers of America (PhRMA)**—www.phrma.org/patients/—Listing of company programs that provide drugs to physicians whose patients could not otherwise afford them.
- **See My Ad Web site**—www.seemyad.com—Site includes description of over 160 private health plans.
- **Social Security Administration**—www.ssa.gov—Information and forms related to programs of the Social Security Administration including SSDI and SSI.
- **State and Local Government on the Net**—www.piperinfo.com/state/index.cfm—Site includes the following for each state:
    - State home page;
    - State and local government telephone directory;
    - Information pertaining to each state's Executive, Legislative, and Judicial Branches; and
    - Information pertaining to county and local offices.
- **TRICARE**—www.tricare.osd.mil—An explanation of health benefits available to dependents of veterans.
- **U.S. Department of Labor**—www.dol.gov/dol/pwba/public/health.htm#related—Site includes information on the following topics:
    - Medicare;
    - State Children's Health Insurance Program;
    - U.S. Dept. of Health and Human Services Consumer Health Links;
    - Federal Employees Health Benefit Plan;
    - State Insurance Departments; and
    - TRICARE Military Health System.
- **Veterans Benefits**—www.va.gov—Site provides information on health benefits available to veterans.

APPENDIX 3

DEFINITION OF KEY ACRONYMS

COBRA—Consolidated Omnibus Budget Reconciliation Act of 1985

This legislation requires that employers as defined in the Act provide employees with continuation of health insurance coverage at group insurance rates when employment is terminated. Whether an employee voluntarily resigns, or is terminated for any reason other than gross misconduct, those employees protected by COBRA must be given the option of continuing their insurance coverage at their own expense for up to 18 months at the group insurance rate. See Chapter 9 for a more detailed explanation.

ERISA—Employee Retirement Income Security Act

ERISA is a federal law that was passed to protect the solvency and security of employee pension plans. However, an unintended benefit of the statute language was to exempt employer health benefit plans from the regulation of state insurance laws if they are self-funded. In self-funded plans, employers set aside revenues to pay the health claims of their workers. Since these benefits are not insurance plans, they are exempt from state insurance laws, including those related to consumer protections. Instead, they are subject to the rules and regulations of the U.S. Department of Labor. Chapter 7 provides a more detailed explanation of ERISA.

HIPAA—Health Insurance Portability and Accountability Act

HIPAA is federal legislation intended to assist individuals when they need to change their group health plan. The law guarantees that most workers who change or lose their jobs will be able to continue to have health insurance without a break in coverage. Eligibility for enrollment in a new group health plan is determined according to the terms of the health plan and the rules of the issuer, and not by the insured's health status or any pre-existing condition. This protection also applies when transferring to individual health insurance coverage. See Chapter 8 for a more detailed explanation.

SSDI—Social Security Disability Insurance

SSDI is an insurance program for workers unable to work due to long-term disability. It is administered by the Social Security Administration and funded by a tax (referred to as the FICA tax) withheld from the worker's pay and by employer contributions. FICA stands for the Federal Income Contribution Act. See Chapter 4 for a more detailed explanation.

SSI—Supplemental Security Income

SSI is a federal income support program administered by the Social Security Administration. It is a government benefit providing a basic monthly income for individuals who are blind, disabled, or 65 years of age or older and meet certain financial thresholds. Unlike Social Security Disability Insurance (SSDI), individuals can receive SSI even if they have never worked or would not otherwise qualify for Social Security. See Chapter 5 for a more detailed explanation.

TWWIIA—Ticket to Work and Work Incentives Improvement Act

TWWIIA was enacted in 1999 to make it easier for people with disabilities who are receiving Social Security Disability to rejoin the workforce without the fear of losing their Medicare coverage. It also provides states with incentives to expand the options and flexibility of their Medicaid programs. See Chapter 11 for a more detailed explanation.

APPENDIX 4

STATE PHARMACEUTICAL ASSISTANCE PROGRAMS

As the cost of pharmaceuticals has continued to rise, states have taken an important role in implementing initiatives to help the elderly and disabled better afford prescription drugs. The most common state pharmaceutical assistance program subsidizes the cost of pharmaceuticals for those who are eligible, requiring the enrollees to pay only a minimal co-pay for their prescriptions. This co-pay typically ranges from $3 to $15. Annual fees, deductibles, and limits on benefits may also be established.

As of Spring 2002, 29 states had enacted laws to create pharmaceutical assistance programs, and three others had programs established through executive branch action. Twenty-six states had programs in operation, and five others had enacted laws but were not in operation yet—Arizona, Arkansas, New Mexico, Oregon, and Wisconsin. While 26 states provide direct subsidy, six additional states have created a discount-only program—California, New Hampshire, Iowa, New Mexico, Washington, and West Virginia. Some states also offer tax credits to assist with the purchase of prescriptions. If Congress provides federal funding to support these programs, it is likely that even more states will offer relief to those struggling with the rising cost of pharmaceuticals.

Income eligibility thresholds for pharmaceutical assistance vary from state to state. States also vary as to whether their program is offered just to the elderly, to the elderly and those who are disabled, or to all residents of limited income.

The following charts, developed by the National Conference of State Legislatures, summarize state pharmaceutical programs in place as of December 2002 for eligible participants. Chart 1 provides brief details on states that provide a state subsidy for the purchase of prescription drugs. Chart 2 describes programs states have been creating recently to provide a reduced or discounted retail price for pharmaceuticals. Please refer to www.ncsl.org/programs/health/drugaid.htm for additional information.

■ State Subsidy Programs (Chart 1)

State	Program Name (*gray shading = operation halted*)	Recipients* = incl. disabled	Eligibility age and maximum income (year) See note about FPL	Year/law citation	Contact/ Telephone/ dates of operation**
Arizona	Prescription Medication Coverage Pilot Program (on-line description)	n/a*	Minimum age: Medicare eligible only Income: $17,720 (200% FPL) (*must reside in a county without HMO prescription drug coverage available*)	2001 S 1118	Not yet operational (*no funds appropriated for 2002*)
Arkansas	Prescription Drug Access Improvement Act (*Medicaid waiver for prescription drug coverage*)	n/a	Minimum age: 65. Income: 90% of FPL ($7,974 in '02), increasing to 100% FPL ($8,860) after 6/30/03. (would provide benefit of 2 Rx per month, only after federal approval is received)	2001: S.932 (signed by Governor 4/16/01)	Not yet operational Dept. of Human Services
California	*Discount program–see chart 2*			1999 SB 393	(*see chart 2*)
Connecticut	Connecticut Pharmaceutical Assistance Contract to the Elderly and the Disabled Program (ConnPACE) (on-line description)	36,352* (FY'02) Disabled (5424)	Minimum age: 65 *effective 4/1/02* Single: $20,000 ('02) Married: $27,100. Disabled: > age 18 on SSI or SSDI (Title 2 or 16)	1986 (sec. 17b-491 et seq.)	EDS: 860-832-9265 In CT: 800-423-5026

STATE PHARMACEUTICAL ASSISTANCE PROGRAMS   173

State	Program Name (gray shading = operation halted)	Recipients* = incl. disabled	Eligibility age and maximum income (year) See note about FPL	Year/law citation	Contact/ Telephone/ dates of operation**
Delaware (1)	Delaware Prescription Drug Assistance Program (DPAP) (on line description) *In effect: 1/14/2000*	5,000 (10/30/02)	Minimum age: 65 Single: $17,720 (200% FPL) Married: $22,128 Disabled: eligible for SSDI	1999 S. 6 of 1999 (Del. Code tit. 16 sec. 3001)	Division of Social Services 800-996-9969 ext. 17 302-577-4900
Delaware (2)	Nemours Health Clinic Pharmaceutical Assistance Program (on-line description)	10,000 ('01)*	Minimum age: 65 Single: $12,500 ('01) Married: $17,125	1981 private initiative	302 651-4405 800 292-9538
District of Columbia	See D.C. below		Income: $17,720; 200% of FPL		
Florida	Ron Silver Senior Drug Program. Prescription Affordability Act (agency description)	36,000 (5/02)	Minimum age: 65 and Dually-Eligible Medicare-Medicaid Individual: $7,974-$10,632 (90%-120% of FPL) effective 7/1/2000 *(part 2 is a discount program for Medicare beneficiaries)*	2000 S 940 2002 H 59	Subsidy program effective 1/1/01 *New program began 7/1/02— see note below* Agency for Health Care Administration 850-414-8306 888 419-3456
Hawaii	*(see discounts, chart 2)*			2002	
Illinois (1)	Pharmaceutical Assistance Program (on-line description)	202,056* (5/16/02)	Minimum age: 65 Single: $22,150 ('02) Married: $29,850 Disabled: over 16. *(see below for changes)*	1985 (320 ILCS 25/4) web link	217-524-0084 In IL: 800 624-2459 Dept. of Revenue

State	Program Name (gray shading = operation halted)	Recipients* = incl. disabled	Eligibility age and maximum income (year) See note about FPL	Year/law citation	Contact/ Telephone/ dates of operation**
Illinois (2)	Illinois Rx SeniorCare (on-line description) Medicaid waiver program	n/a (est. eligible 368,000 incl. Existing persons moved from PAP)	Minimum age: 65 Single: $17,720 Couple: $23,880 ('02)	2001: Public Act 92-0010—see 305 ILCS 5/5–5.12a	Enrollment open 6/02 Dept. of Revenue Enroll: 800-252-8966
Indiana	"HoosierRx" Indiana Prescription Drug Fund (on-line description)	15,422 (4/02) (est. 66,000 eligible)	Minimum age: 65 Single: $12,758 (9/02) (144% FPL) Couple: $16,128 (135% FPL Net Income after Medicaid premiums) 50% discount/ cash refunds $20million appropriated	2000: S. 108, sec. 6 (signed 3/13/00) 2002 change S 228 sec. 38	Began 10/00 317-234-1381 In IN: 866-267-4679
Iowa	(see discounts, chart 2)			(not in law)	
Kansas	Senior Pharmacy Assistance Program (on-line description)	1,147 (11/02)	Minimum age: 67 Single: up to 135% of poverty $11,961 ('02) Married: $16,119 Must bedual-eligible— see notes. Copayment: 30%; maximum reimbursement: $1,200 per person.	2000 HB 2814 (signed 5/16/2000)	Effective date 7/1/2001; funding extended to 6/30/03. Dept. of Aging 785-368-7327
Maine (1)	Healthy Maine Prescription Program (on-line description) (includes subsidy & Medicaid waiver)	36,000 subsidy + 79,000 discount only; total 115,000* (9/1/02)	Income limit: Medicare enrollees up to 300% FPL. Single: $26,580. HCFA granted Medicaid waiver, 1/19/2001 See NCSL report: Prescription Drug Laws in Maine	1975 36 M.R.S. sec. 6161 2001 LD 1790 (signed 5/25/01)	Law effective 6/1/01 888-600-2466 207-287-2674 (court action pending)

STATE PHARMACEUTICAL ASSISTANCE PROGRAMS ■ 175

State	Program Name (*gray shading = operation halted*)	Recipients* = incl. disabled	Eligibility age and maximum income (year) *See note about FPL*	Year/law citation	Contact/ Telephone/ dates of operation**
Maine (1a)	Low Cost Drugs for the Elderly Program (on-line description)	Transferred to new program 41,000 (5/01)	Minimum age: 62 Single: $15,244 (3/01) Married: $20,461 — If 40% of income goes to drugs: Single: $19,185 Married: $25,575 Disabled: age 55+	1975 36 M.R.S. sec. 6161–6166	Program ended 6/1/01, enrollees transferred to Healthy Maine Program
Maine (2)	Maine Rx Program (*see discounts, chart 2*)				
Maryland (1)	Maryland Pharmacy Assistance Program	35,901* ('01) Budget $37.3m	Minimum age: no limit Single: $10,000 Married: $10,850 Disabled: yes No limitation by age or medical condition. $4500 max. assets	1979 (Health- General sec. 15–124) web link	Sec. Of Health & Mental Hygiene 410-767-5394 800-492-1974
Maryland (2)	CareFirst Plan Also known as: Short-Term Prescription Drug Subsidy Plan	1,700* (7/1/01) (*max. of 30,000, to end 7/03*)	Minimum age: 65 or Medicare eligible. Single: $25,770 Married: $34,830 $1000 annual benefit limit	2000 SB.855; Chapter 565; + 2001 HB.6/ SB 236; Chapter 135 (signed 4/20/01)	(new features in effect 6/30/01) 410-767-5394 800-492-1974
Massachu- setts (1)	Prescription Advantage Plan (on-line description) Subsidized Prescription Drug Insurance Program	83,000* (8/1/02)	Minimum age: 65 No upper income limit; No premium or deductibles under 188% of FPL ($16,668); sliding scale premium & deductible subsidy up to 500% FPL ($44,300) ('02) Disabled: $16,668.	(MGL 19A sec. 39, 40) 2001 H.4900 sec. 11 11/01, amended Emergency Reg.	Exec. Office of Elder Affairs 617-727-7750 customer service 800-243-4636

176 ■ APPENDIX FOUR

State	Program Name (gray shading = operation halted)	Recipients* = incl. disabled	Eligibility age and maximum income (year) See note about FPL	Year/law citation	Contact/ Telephone/ dates of operation**
Massachusetts (1a)	The Pharmacy Program (on-line description) formerly Senior Pharmacy Assistance Program	47,000 (7/01)	Minimum age: 65 Single: $15,708 ('00) Married: $21,156 (*see above for 2001 expansions*)	1996 (Ch. 118E, sec.16B & Chapter 170 of 1997)	Program ended 9/30/01, (replaced by Plan #1 above)
Michigan (1)	Elder Prescription Insurance Coverage (EPIC) Program (on-line description)	15,000 (enrollees from priority enrollment opportunity) (Less than 200 people have emergency coverage) (5/3/02)	Minimum age: 65 Single: $17,720 (200% FPL) Married: $23,880 Annual fee of $25 For 45 day emergency coverage (150% FPL) Single: $13,290 Married: $17,910	2000	In operation Oct. 1, 2001 toll-free: 866-747-5844 For policy information, MI Dept. of Community Health 517-373-2559
Michigan (2)	Michigan Emergency Pharmaceutical Program for Seniors (MEPPS)	12,000 ('01)	Minimum age: 65 Single: $12,885/yr. ('01) Married: $17,415/yr. (*Monthly drug expenses of at least 10% of monthly income for singles.*)	1988 & 1994	Program ended 9/30/01 (enrollees given priority to enter EPIC program and eligible for benefits 12/01/01)
Michigan (3) see (#1) and note below	Prescription Drug Credit Program (Income tax credit) (on-line description)	31,000 est.	Minimum age: 65 Single: $12,885 Family: $17,415 (150% FPL) Tax credit up to $600 for prescriptions over 5% of household income	1988	MI Dept. of Community Health (Program ended 12/31/01, recipients to be rolled over into EPIC)
Minnesota	Prescription Drug Program In effect Jan. 1999 (on-line description)	4,573 (4/02)	Minimum age: 65 Single: $10,632/yr Couple: $14,328/yr ('02) (*liquid assets under $10,000 or $18,000 couple*)	1997–Ch. 225, Art 4 (statute sec. 256.955)	Dept. of Human Services 651-297-5404 Senior Linkage Line: 800-333-2433

STATE PHARMACEUTICAL ASSISTANCE PROGRAMS ■ 177

State	Program Name (gray shading = operation halted)	Recipients* = incl. disabled	Eligibility age and maximum income (year) See note about FPL	Year/law citation	Contact/ Telephone/ dates of operation**
Missouri (1)	Missouri Senior Rx Program (on-line description)	29,500 (11/02)	Minimum age: Single: $17,000 Couple: $23,000 Co-pay = 40%; $250-500 deductible, depending on income. Application fee $25-35 /year.	2001: HB 3 & SB 4 signed 10/5/01	Operational: 7/1/02 Info: 866-556-9316
Missouri (2)	Pharmaceutical Tax Credit (*State income tax credit for legend drugs*) In effect Aug. 1999	262,000 (*see note below*)	Minimum age: 65 Single: up to $15,000 = $200 credit. Credit reduced by $2 for each $100 income.	1999 S14	573-751-4081 (Program ended 12/1/01; replaced by Rx above)
Nevada	Senior Rx Insurance Subsidy for Prescription Drugs (On-line description)	7,500 (11/02) Currently 1,100 waiting for enrollment.	Minimum age: 62 Family: $21,500 (*subsidy for prescription drugs private insurance policies; uses tobacco funds*)	1999 & 2001 SB 539 signed 6/5/01 as Ch. 529	Operational as of 1/1/2001 Department of Human Resources, Director Inside NV: 800-262-7726
New Hampshire	(*see discounts, chart 2*)			(*not in law*)	
New Jersey (1)	PAAD— Pharmaceutical Assistance for the Aged and Disabled (on-line description)	195,866* (5/02)	Minimum age: 65 Single: $19,739 Married: $24,203 Disabled: age 21 ('02) $5 copayment	1975 (Ch.30: 4D–20 et seq.) web link	Dept. of Health & Senior Services 609-588-7048 In NJ: 800-792-9745
New Jersey (2)	Senior Gold Prescription Discount Program (on-line description)	(*included above*)	Minimum age: 65 Single: $19,739–$29,739 Married:$23,204–$34,203 ('02) 50% co-payment (*Adjusts each January*)	2001 S.6; Ch. 96 of 2001 (signed 5/15/01)	609-588-7048 In NJ: 800-792-9745

178 ■ APPENDIX FOUR

State	Program Name (*gray shading = operation halted*)	Recipients* = incl. disabled	Eligibility age and maximum income (year) *See note about FPL*	Year/law citation	Contact/ Telephone/ dates of operation**
New Mexico	(*see discounts, chart 2*)			2002	
New York	EPIC—Elderly Pharmaceutical Insurance Coverage (on-line description)	297,000 (11/02)	Minimum age: 65 Single: $35,000 Married: $50,000 ('02)	1987 law (Executive 19-K sec. 547 et seq.) web link	518-452-6828 In NY: 800-332-3742
North Carolina (1)	Prescription Drug Assistance Program (on-line description) Enrollment was closed 3/01 due to budget limitations— *see notes*	1,710 (5/6/02)	Minimum Age: 65 Single: $13,290 ('02) 150% of poverty level For persons diagnosed with heart disease (CVD) or diabetes.	1999— H 168 (Part XI, Ch. 237 of 1999) web link	Began operation May 2000 Public Health Dept. 919-715-3338 NC Care Line: 800-662-7030
North Carolina (2)	North Carolina Senior Care Health Plan (online description)	4,100 (11/1/02) (100,000 expected by '03)	Minimum Age: 65 Single: $17,180 Married: $23,220 (11/02) (*Up to 200% FLP for 2001*) For persons diagnosed with heart disease (CVD), COPD, or diabetes.	2001 Decision	Benefits begin 11/02 Toll-free: 866-226-1388
Ohio	(*see discounts, chart 2*)				Dept of Aging
Oregon	Senior Prescription Drug Assistance Program (*Also, see discounts, chart 2*)	n/a (100,000 estimated eligible)	Minimum age: 65 Max. income: 185% FPL Single: $16,391 Couple: $22,089 Max. assets of $2000; no other private or public drug benefit program in pervious 6 mo. annual benefit cap of $2000; max. subsidy of 50% per prescription. Cost of card: $50 annually.	2001 SB 9 (signed 7/30/01)	Not yet in operation; postponed due to lack of funds** Estimated rollout Feb. '03. Dept of Human Services 503-945-6530

STATE PHARMACEUTICAL ASSISTANCE PROGRAMS ■ 179

State	Program Name (gray shading = operation halted)	Recipients* = incl. disabled	Eligibility age and maximum income (year) See note about FPL	Year/law citation	Contact/ Telephone/ dates of operation**
Pennsylvania (1)	PACE— Pharmaceutical Assistance for the Elderly on-line link	192,000 (11/02)	Minimum age: 65 Single: $14,000 ('01) Married: $17,200	1984, P.L.351, No. 91 sec. 502 (72 PS sec. 3761–501 to 709)	PA Dept. of Aging 717-652-9028 In PA: 800-225-7223
Pennsylvania (2)	PACENET— PACE Needs Enhancement Tier on-line link	31,000 (11/02)	Minimum age: 65 Single: $16,000 ('01) Married: to $19,200	1996 P.L. 741, No. 134	PA Dept. of Aging 717-652-9028 In PA: 800 225-7223
Rhode Island	RIPAE— Rhode Island Pharmaceutical Assistance for the Elderly (on-line description)	33,000 (7/01)	Minimum age: 65 Single: $16,490–$36,225 ('01) Married: $20,613–$41,400 Program has 3 levels of coverage, based on income. *Excludes income spent on medical expenses if greater than 3% of total income.*	1985 (sec. 42-66.2–5) web link + 2000 expansion started 7/01	Dept. of Elderly Affairs 401-222-2880 (within the state) 222-2880
South Carolina	SilverxCard— Seniors' Prescription Drug Program (on-line description)	40,000 (7/02)	Minimum age: 65 Single: $15,505 Married: $20,895 ('02) will expand in 2003. Requires $500 /yr. Deductible & $10–$21 copayments	2000 H.3699 Act 406 of 2000 5/19/00	Operational 1/1/2001 Office of Insurance Services 877-239-5277 803-734-1061
Texas (1)	State Prescription Drug Program (on-line description)	n/a	Eligibility: Medicare dual-eligibles and others; upper limit to be determined by Commission	2001: HB 1094 (signed 6/15/01)	Not yet in operation; postponed due to lack of funds

180 ■ APPENDIX FOUR

State	Program Name (gray shading = operation halted)	Recipients* = incl. disabled	Eligibility age and maximum income (year) See note about FPL	Year/law citation	Contact/ Telephone/ dates of operation**
Vermont (1)	VHAP Pharmacy— Vermont Health Access Program Covers acute care and maintenance drugs (Medicaid funded via 1115 waiver) (online description)	11,550* (11/02)	Minimum age: 65 150% FPL Single: $13,368 ('02) Married: $17,988 Disabled: Recipients of disability benefits through SS or Medicare	1996 Act 14 of 1996, sec. 14 + HCFA 1115 waiver	800-529-4060 (in state) 800-250-8427 (out of state)
Vermont (2)	VSCRIPT Covers only maintenance drugs (online description)	3,011* (12/01)	Minimum age: 65 or disabled 175% FPL Single: $15,600 ('02) Married: $20,988 Disabled: Recipients of Social Security	1989 (33 VSA sec. 1991–1994) (as expanded by sec. 122–123 of Act 62 of 1999)	800-529-4060 (in state) 800-250-8427 (out of state)
Vermont (3)	VSCRIPT Expanded Covers only maintenance drugs (online description)	3,187* (11/02)	Minimum age: 65 or disabled 225% FPL Single: $20,052 ('02) Married: $26,988	Approved Jan '00	800-529-4060 (in state) 800-250-8427 (out of state)
Vermont (4)	(see discounts, chart 2)				
Washington	(see discounts, chart 2)				
West Virginia	(see discounts, chart 2)				

State	Program Name (gray shading = operation halted)	Recipients* = incl. disabled	Eligibility age and maximum income (year) See note about FPL	Year/law citation	Contact/ Telephone/ dates of operation**
Wisconsin	Wisconsin SeniorCare Prescription Drug Assistance Program Prescription Drug Assistance for Elderly Persons	42,000 (9/02)	Minimum age: 65 Income: up to 240% of FPL (starting at $14,176 per individual and $19,104 per couple annually, capped at $21,265 or higher per individual and $28,657 or higher per couple annually). Enrollment fee $20	2001 SB55, excerpt (signed 8/31/01)	SeniorCare Customer Service Hotline 800-657-2038 or call the local aging agency
Wyoming (1)	Prescription Drug Assistance Program	1,234* (7/01– 10/01)	Minimum age: no limit Income: $8,860 100% of federal poverty ('02) and no more than $1000 in resources (home and 1 car exempt)	2002 S 34, signed 3/11/02	Dept of Health/ Medicaid 307-777-7531 800-442-2766
Wyoming (1a)	Minimum Medical Program *(Has been absorbed into the new program.)* (online description)	740* average per month (5/02)	Minimum age: no limit Income: $8,860; 100% of federal poverty level. ('02)	1988 (Dept. of Health regulations)	Dept of Health/ Medicaid 307-777-7531 800-442-2766

* = program includes adult disabled

** = dates of operation for new programs are based on statute; actual implementation schedules may vary based on agency administrative practices.

State Pharmaceutical Discount Programs (Chart 2)

State	Discount Program Name	Recipients* = incl. disabled	Eligibility age & maximum income (year)	Year/law citation or authority	Contact/ Telephone/ dates of operation**
Arkansas	See recent actions below			See AR below	
California (1)	Discount Prescription Medication Program (*retail discounts via pharmacies— see on-line description*)	n/a* (*est. 1.3 million eligible*)	Medicare recipients, 65 or disabled; no income limit In effect: 2/1/2000	1999 SB 393; 2001 SB 696	Dept. of Health Services 916-657-4302 HICAP: 800-434-0222
California (1a)	Golden Bear State Pharmacy Assistance Program (*revised structure for Discount Program, above*)	n/a*	Medicare recipients, 65 or disabled; no income limit (*Requires manufacturer rebates to achieve larger discounts*)	2001 SB 696	Not yet in effect Medi-Cal 916-657-1280
Connecticut (2)	ConnPACE part "B"	n/a*	Not specified in law	2000 Public Act 00–2)	Not in operation
Florida (2)	Prescription Discount Program (on-line description) (*also see subsidy description in chart 1*)	n/a* enrollment not required	Any Medicare beneficiary, no age or income limit. *Discounts based on Average Wholesale Price minus 9% + $4.50 dispensing fee, provided by retail pharmacies*	2000 S 940 (*see chart 1*)	Effective 7/1/00 AHCA: 850-487-4441 888-419-3456
Hawaii (1)	Hawaii Rx discount program	n/a*	Age: "All residents of the state shall be eligible." Income: no limit.	2002 HB 2834 law effective 7/1/02	Not yet operational goal 7/1/04
Hawaii (2)	Medicaid Prescription Drug Expansion Program	n/a*	Age: no limit. Eligibility: income up up to $30,600 individual; couple = $41,220 ('02)	2002 HB 1950 law effective 7/1/02	Not yet operational (*Requires federal waiver*)

STATE PHARMACEUTICAL ASSISTANCE PROGRAMS ■ 183

State	Discount Program Name	Recipients* = incl. disabled	Eligibility age & maximum income (year)	Year/law citation or authority	Contact/ Telephone/ dates of operation**
Iowa	Iowa Priority Prescription Savings Program (on-line description) *(originally Iowa Prescription Drug Purchasing Cooperative)*	24,000 (9/1/02)	Eligibility: any Medicare beneficiary. *($20 annual enrollment; discounts only)* Start-up via HCFA federal grant news story, 11/8/01	(not in state law)	Enrollment open 11/10/01; operational 1/2/02 Dept of Public Health 515-281-4343 toll-free 866-282-5817
Maine (1b) *Also see chart 1*	Healthy Maine Prescription Program Medicaid Waiver benefit (on-line description) *(discount program with subsidy)*	79,000 discount only; state total 115,000 *See chart 1*	Income limit: Medicare enrollees up to 300% of FPL. $26,580. HCFA granted Medicaid waiver, 1/19/2001	2001 Chapter 293 (signed 5/25/01)	In operation 6/1/01 888-600-2466 207-287-2674 *(court action on waiver is pending)*
Maine (2)	Maine Rx Program *(discount prices, based on Medicaid & manufacturer rebates)* (on-line details) *(agency update)*	n/a* (325,000 estimated eligible in '01)	Minimum age: none All Maine residents with an Rx enrollment card *See NCSL report: Prescription Drug Laws in Maine*	2000 S.1026; Chapter 786, sec. 2681 (signed 5/11/2000)	Not implemented due to legal challenge Law provided for operation to begin 1/1/01 207-287-2674 Bureau of Medical Services
Maryland (3)	Maryland Pharmacy Discount Program *(also see subsidies in chart 1)*	n/a* (est. future participation 105,000)	Income limit: 250% of FPL; if federal waiver: none Medicare beneficiaries 65 and over; also disabled.	HB.6; Chapter 134 & 135 (signed 4/20/01)	Law effective 7/1/01 discounts operational; goal 1/1/02
Massachu- setts (2)	Aggregate Purchasing law	n/a	State agency to coordinate combined purchasing for Senior Pharmacy Assistance enrollees, Medicare and Medicaid, state workers, uninsured and underinsured people.	Chapter 127 of 1999 sec. 271 (signed 11/99) also see H.4900 sec. 11 (2001)	Not in operation— delayed by Executive branch

184 ■ APPENDIX FOUR

State	Discount Program Name	Recipients* = incl. disabled	Eligibility age & maximum income (year)	Year/law citation or authority	Contact/ Telephone/ dates of operation**
Massachusetts (3)	Pharmacy Outreach Program, known as "Mass. MedLine" (online description)	n/a	Any resident may obtain advice from academic pharmacist + help w/ industry program applications at no charge.	2000: Sec. 45 of H.5300	Executive Office of Elder Affairs 508-373-0031 toll-free: 866-633-1617
New Hampshire	Prescription Drug Discount Program for Seniors (online description)	Est. 12,000 (2/02)	Minimum age: 65 no income limit No enrollment fee	2000 (not in law)	Pilot program began 1/2000. Division of Elderly and Adult Services 800-351-1888
New Mexico	Senior Prescription Drug Program	n/a	Minimum age: 65 no income limit (*provides discount as negotiated by state agency*)	2002: SB 91 & HB 200 signed 3/5/02	Not yet operational NM Retiree Health Care Authority
Ohio	Golden Buckeye Card Program	n/a (est. up to 500,000)	Minimum age: 60 Disabled: no age limit no income limit fees allowed but not yet established	2002 SB 261, sec. 173.06 signed 6/5/02	Not yet operational goal: early 2003 Dept of Aging
Oregon	Senior Prescription Drug Assistance Program— discounts	(est. up to 100,000)	Minimum age 65 (*provides a discount not to exceed Medicaid Rx rate*) Eligibility up to $16,391 (185% FPL); Enrollment $50 annually		Not yet operational; estimated 11/02 503-945-6530
Texas (2)	Interagency Council on Pharmaceuticals Bulk Purchasing	n/a	Combines Health Dept., public employees, and all other state programs. Council "shall develop procedures that member agencies must follow in purchasing pharmaceuticals."	2001: HB 915 (signed 6/15/01)	Not yet operational

STATE PHARMACEUTICAL ASSISTANCE PROGRAMS ■ 185

State	Discount Program Name	Recipients* = incl. disabled	Eligibility age & maximum income (year)	Year/law citation or authority	Contact/ Telephone/ dates of operation**
Vermont (4)	Healthy Vermonters Discount Program (*Includes a Medicaid waiver provision and a 2% state payment toward cost of drugs*)	n/a*	Minimum age: none If age 65+, income: up to 400% FPL ($35,440 individual; $47,760 couple) Disabled: SSDI; Other under 65: 300% FPL.	H.31 of 2002 Signed 6/13/02 as Act 127	Law effective 7/1/02 Discount not yet operational
Vermont (4a)	Pharmacy Discount Program (PDP); expansion of VHAP, above (online description) (*provides for retail discount only; no state subsidy*)	3,026* (3/01) (est. eligible 69,000)	Medicaid benefit: Minimum age: none any Medicare-covered individual; others w/o coverage Single: $25,056 Couple: $33,756	2000: H 842 section 117	HCFA waiver approved 11/00 Began 1/1/2001 Federal court ruling 6/8/01 halted operation
Washington	A Washington Alliance to Reduce Prescription-Drug Spending (*retail discount only*)	5,000 (5/01)	Minimum age: 55 no income limit $15 annual enrollment charge	(Not in law) Executive Order 00–04 WAC 246–30 signed 8/29/00	Began 3/19/01 Program invalidated and terminated. 6/01 enrollees transferred to private sector program, June, 2001.*
West Virginia (1)	SPAN II (*retail discount only*)	4,000 (7/15/01) moved to GM card, below	Minimum age: 65 Eligibility: No income requirement as of 4/01, WV resident, no enrollment fee	(Not in law) Executive order 20–00 signed 10/18/00	Began 12/00 Phased out, fall 2001 877-987-4463 or 877-987-2622
West Virginia (2)	Golden Mountaineer Discount Card Program (online description)	13,809 (12/31/01)	Minimum age: 60 Eligibility: no income requirements		Began 9/01 Bureau of Senior Services 304-558-3317 or toll-free at 1-877-987-3646

n/a = enrollment or participation figures not yet available for new programs.

APPENDIX 5

STATE CHILDREN'S HEALTH INSURANCE PROGRAM

In 1997, Congress adopted legislation to assist states in providing health insurance coverage to children from working families with incomes too high to qualify for Medicaid but too low to afford private insurance. Titled the State Children's Health Insurance Program, or SCHIP, each state with an approved plan receives federal matching funds for its plan's expenditures. As of May, 2002, all 50 states, the District of Columbia, and five U.S. territories have programs that have been approved by the federal Department of Health and Human Services.

The legislation sets eligibility criteria while providing each state discretionary authority to narrow the standard for those children targeted to be covered under its program. In most states, children are eligible for SCHIP coverage if:

- They are uninsured, living in working families with low or moderate incomes (i.e., a family of four with an income not exceeding $36,200 per year would be eligible in most states);
- They are under the age of 19; and

Although benefits vary from state to state, children generally are eligible for:

- Regular checkups;
- Immunization;
- Eyeglasses;
- Doctor visits;
- Prescription drug coverage; and
- Hospital care.

The premiums charged by a state must be based on an income-related sliding scale.

A status report and contact information regarding State Children's Health Insurance Programs is obtained from the web site of the Center for Medicare and Medicaid Services—www.cms.gov.

Index

acronyms and abbreviations, definition of, 169–170
administrative law judge (ALJ) and appeals, Social Security Disability Insurance (SSDI) and, 40–41
Agency for Healthcare Research and Quality, 165
Alabama
   high-risk insurance pool requirements, regulations for, 94–95
   telephone numbers for health/long-term care insurance help in, 143
Alaska
   grievance and appeals process in, 11
   high-risk insurance pool requirements, regulations for, 95–97
   Supplemental Security Income (SSI) and Medicaid coverage rules in, 49
   telephone numbers for health/long-term care insurance help in, 143–144
application process (SSDI/SSI)
   description of disability in, with worksheet, 53–56
   forms required in, and filing process, 57–58
   physician contacts checklist for, 57
   Social Security Disability Insurance (SSDI) and, 38–39, 53–58
   Supplemental Security Income (SSI) and, 47
   work history checklist for, 57
Arizona
   telephone numbers for health/long-term care insurance help in, 144
Arkansas
   high-risk insurance pool requirements, regulations for, 98–99

Arkansas (continued)
   mini-COBRA regulations in, 80
   telephone numbers for health/long-term care insurance help in, 144
attorney fees for application
   Social Security Disability Insurance (SSDI) and, 42–43
   Supplemental Security Income (SSI) and, 51
attorneys and counsel during application process
   Social Security Disability Insurance (SSDI) and, 41–42
   Supplemental Security Income (SSI) and, 50–51

California
   grievance and appeals process in, 11–12
   high-risk insurance pool requirements, regulations for, 99–101
   mini-COBRA regulations in, 80
   telephone numbers for health/long-term care insurance help in, 145
capitated basis managed care organization (MCO), Medicaid and, 34–35
Center for Medicare Advocacy, 165
Center for Medicare and Medicaid Services, 165
certificate of coverage
   Consolidated Omnibus Budget Reconciliation Act of 1985 (COBRA) and, 77
   Health Insurance Portability and Accountability Act (HIPAA) and, 65–66
challenging an adverse decisions, 13–14

checklist for health insurance policy selection, 18–19
children's health insurance program (SCHIP), 165, 187–188
claim appeal letter, sample, 15–16
COBRA (See Consolidated Omnibus Reconciliation Act of 1985), 21
co-insurance, 7
  Consolidated Omnibus Budget Reconciliation Act of 1985 (COBRA) and, 74
Colorado
  high-risk insurance pool requirements, regulations for, 101–102
  mini-COBRA regulations in, 80
  telephone numbers for health/long-term care insurance help in, 145
Connecticut
  high-risk insurance pool requirements, regulations for, 103–104
  mini-COBRA regulations in, 80
  Supplemental Security Income (SSI) and Medicaid coverage rules in, 49
  telephone numbers for health/long-term care insurance help in, 145–146
Consolidated Omnibus Budget Reconciliation Act of 1985 (COBRA), 19, 21, 71–77
  certificate of coverage and, 77
  core and non-core benefits under, 74–75
  cost of coverage under, 76
  covered benefits under, 73–75
  deductibles and co-insurance under, 74
  dependent children defined for, 72–73
  election period for, 76
  employee defined under, 71
  ERISA and, 79
  exempted individuals under, 71–72
  Health Insurance Portability and Accountability Act (HIPAA) and, 66, 67
  health maintenance organizations (HMO) and, 74
  HIPAA and, 77
  identical coverage benefit under, 73–74
  mini-COBRAs and, 79–90
  notice by disabled beneficiaries of, 76
  notice by the employee of, 75–76
  notice by the employer of, 75–76

Consolidated Omnibus Budget Reconciliation Act of 1985 (COBRA) (continued)
  options and limitations of plans under, 74
  preferred provider organization (PPO) and, 74
  qualifying event defined under, 71, 72–73
  state high-risk insurance pools and, 93
Cooperative of Home Care Associates (CHCA), 21
cooperatives, health care coverage, 21
co-pay, 7

deductible, 7–8
  Consolidated Omnibus Budget Reconciliation Act of 1985 (COBRA) and, 74
defined contribution plans, 20–21
Delaware
  grievance and appeals process in, 12
  telephone numbers for health/long-term care insurance help in, 146
Department of Labor, 61, 168
dependent children, under COBRA, 72–73
directory, state telephone numbers for health and long-term care insurance, 143–163
disability, description of, with worksheet, 53–56
District of Columbia
  telephone numbers for health/long-term care insurance help in, 146
Duke Center for Health Policy, Law, and Management, 165

earned income exclusion for Medicaid, 35
Employee Retirement Income Security Act (ERISA)
  appeals and disputes under, 60–62
  COBRA and, 79
  Department of Labor's role in, 61
  grievance and appeals process in, 10–11, 16, 59–62
  Norwood–Dingle bill and, 60
  Patient Protection Act and, 60
  pre–emption under, 59–62
employer sponsored plans, 21
employment status and Medicaid, 35
external review, state, 16

Families USA, 165
fee for service (indemnity) plans, 2–3
 managed care and vs., 9–10
 Medicare and, 25–27
FICA tax funding of SSDI, 37
Florida
 high-risk insurance pool requirements, regulations for, 104–105
 mini-COBRA regulations in, 81
 telephone numbers for health/long-term care insurance help in, 146–147
formularies, open and closed, 8
Franklin Health Assurance Company, 1
fraud, 68–69

gatekeepers, 6
Georgetown University Medical Center Health Care Research and Policy, 166
Georgia
 mini-COBRA regulations in, 81
 telephone numbers for health/long-term care insurance help in, 147
Google search engine, 166
GovSpot, 166
grievance and appeals process, 10–16
 challenging an adverse decision in, 13–14
 Employee Retirement Income Security Act (ERISA) and, 10–11, 16, 60–62
 external review, state, 16
 sample claim appeal letter, 15–16
 Social Security Disability Insurance (SSDI) and, 39–42
 state regulations pertaining to, 11–14
 Supplemental Security Income (SSI) and, 48–49
group model HMO, 5

Hawaii
 grievance and appeals process in, 12
 Supplemental Security Income (SSI) and Medicaid coverage rules in, 49
 telephone numbers for health/long-term care insurance help in, 147–148
health care fraud, 68–69
Health Hippo, 166
Health Insurance Association of America (HIAA), 166
Health Insurance Glossary, 166

Health Insurance Portability and Accountability Act (HIPAA), 7, 19, 21, 63–69
 certificate of coverage and, 65–66
 Consolidated Omnibus Budget Reconciliation Act of 1985 (COBRA) and, 66, 67, 77
 eligibility for, 64–65
 fraud and, 68–69
 guaranteed protections under, 63–64
 long term care insurance and, 67
 Medical Savings Accounts (MSA) and, 67–68
 non-discrimination based on health status and, 65
 pre-existing conditions and, 6–7, 64–65, 69
 privacy regulations under, 69
 state modification and pre–emption of, 66
 state modifications to, 7
health maintenance organization (HMO), 2, 4–6
 Consolidated Omnibus Budget Reconciliation Act of 1985 (COBRA) and, 74
 group model, 5
 individual practice association (IPA), 5–6
 Medicare and, 25–26
 network model, 5
 staff model, 4–5
Health Maintenance Organization Act of 1973, 2
Health Finder, 166
high-risk insurance pools (*See* state high-risk insurance pools)
HIPAA (*See* Health Insurance Portability and Accountability Act)
history of health insurance, 1–2

Idaho
 Supplemental Security Income (SSI) and Medicaid coverage rules in, 49
 telephone numbers for health/long-term care insurance help in, 148
Illinois
 Employee Retirement Income Security Act (ERISA) and, 62
 high-risk insurance pool requirements, regulations for, 106–107
 mini-COBRA regulations in, 81

Illinois (continued)
   Supplemental Security Income (SSI) and Medicaid coverage rules in, 49
   telephone numbers for health/long-term care insurance help in, 148
impairment–related work expenses and Medicaid, 35
indemnity plans (*See also* fee for service plans), 2–3
Independent Living Centers, 166
Indiana
   high-risk insurance pool requirements, regulations for, 108–109
   Supplemental Security Income (SSI) and Medicaid coverage rules in, 49
   telephone numbers for health/long-term care insurance help in, 149
individual practice association (IPA), 5–6
Insure.com, 166
Iowa
   high-risk insurance pool requirements, regulations for, 109–111
   mini-COBRA regulations in, 81–82
   telephone numbers for health/long-term care insurance help in, 149

Kaiser Foundation Health Plan, 5
Kansas
   high-risk insurance pool requirements, regulations for, 112–113
   mini-COBRA regulations in, 82
   Supplemental Security Income (SSI) and Medicaid coverage rules in, 49
   telephone numbers for health/long-term care insurance help in, 149–150
Kassebaum–Kennedy Bill (*See also* Health Insurance Portability and Accountability Act), 63
Kentucky
   grievance and appeals process in, 12
   high-risk insurance pool requirements, regulations for, 113–114
   mini-COBRA regulations in, 82
   telephone numbers for health/long-term care insurance help in, 150

lifetime maximum, 8

long-term care insurance (*See also* individual state entries), Health Insurance Portability and Accountability Act (HIPAA) and, 67
Los Angeles Department of Water and Power, 2
Louisiana
   high-risk insurance pool requirements, regulations for, 115–116
   mini-COBRA regulations in, 82
   telephone numbers for health/long-term care insurance help in, 150–151

Maine
   grievance and appeals process in, 13
   mini-COBRA regulations in, 83
   telephone numbers for health/long-term care insurance help in, 151
managed care, 3–18
   advantages and disadvantages of, 15–17
   choosing a physician under, 9
   co-insurance and co-pay in, 7
   deductible in, 7–8
   definitions, terms, and features of, 6–8
   Employee Retirement Income Security Act (ERISA) and, 10, 16, 59–62
   formularies in, open and closed, 8
   gatekeepers in, 6
   grievance and appeals process under, 10–16
   health insurance policy checklist for, 18–19
   lifetime maximum in, 8
   maximum out of pocket amount in, 8
   Medicaid and, 33–36
   Medicare and, 25–26
   monitoring member satisfaction with, 10
   open enrollment in, 8
   payment methods under, 9
   periodic check ups under, 9
   pre–existing condition in, 6–7
   premium in, 8
   primary care physician (PCP) in, 4, 6, 16, 17
   prior authorization in, 8
   quality and qualifications of physicians under, 9
   sources of potential insurance coverage in, 20–21
   specialist consultations under, 9

managed care (continued)
   state modifications to HIPAA and, 7
   tips for, 19–20
   traditional (indemnity) plans vs., 9–10
managed care organization (MCO), 9
Managed Health Care Glossary, 167
Maryland
   grievance and appeals process in, 13
   mini-COBRA regulations in, 83
   telephone numbers for health/long-term care insurance help in, 151
Massachusetts
   grievance and appeals process in, 13
   mini-COBRA regulations in, 83
   telephone numbers for health/long-term care insurance help in, 151–152
maximum out of pocket amount, 8
Medicaid, 31–36
   capitated basis managed care organization (MCO) and, 34–35
   earned income exclusion for, 35
   eligibility requirements for, 31–32
   employment status and, 35
   impairment–related work expenses and, 35
   managed care and, 33–36
   plan for achieving self–support (PASS) and, 36
   primary care case management (PCCM) program and, 34
   Section 1619b continued eligibility requirements for, 36
   services covered by, 32–33
   Supplemental Security Income Program (SSI) and, 31–32
   ticket to work and work incentives improvement act and, 36, 91–92
Medical Savings Accounts (MSA), Health Insurance Portability and Accountability Act (HIPAA) and, 67–68
Medicare, 23–30
   demonstration project for fee for service plans under, 26–27
   fee for service (indemnity) plans and, 25, 26–27
   financial assistance for costs of, 28
   fraud and, 68–69
   Medigap (Medicare Supplemental Insurance) and, 28–30
   Part A coverage under, 23–24

Medicare (continued)
   Part B coverage under, 24–25
   Part C coverage (managed care option) under, 25–26
   preferred provider organizations (PPO) and, 25–27
   services not covered under, 26–27
   skilled nursing care under, 24
   Social Security Disability (SSD) and, 23–24
   Social Security Disability Insurance (SSDI) and, 43
   Web sites of interest to, 167
Medicare Rights Center, 167
Medigap (Medicare Supplemental Insurance) and, 28–30
Michigan
   grievance and appeals process in, 13
   telephone numbers for health/long-term care insurance help in, 152
mini-COBRAs, 19, 79–90
Minnesota
   high-risk insurance pool requirements, regulations for, 116–118
   mini-COBRA regulations in, 83–84
   Supplemental Security Income (SSI) and Medicaid coverage rules in, 49
   telephone numbers for health/long-term care insurance help in, 152
Mississippi
   high-risk insurance pool requirements, regulations for, 118–119
   mini-COBRA regulations in, 84
   telephone numbers for health/long-term care insurance help in, 153
Missouri
   high-risk insurance pool requirements, regulations for, 119–121
   mini-COBRA regulations in, 84
   Supplemental Security Income (SSI) and Medicaid coverage rules in, 49
   telephone numbers for health/long-term care insurance help in, 153
Montana
   high-risk insurance pool requirements, regulations for, 121–123
   telephone numbers for health/long-term care insurance help in, 153–154
Montgomery Ward and Co. health insurance, 2

National Aging Administration Center, 167
National Association of Insurance Commissioners, 167
National Governor's Association, 2
national health insurance, 2
National Health Law Program, 167
National Library of Medicine, 167
National Organization of Social Security Claimant Representatives (NOSSCR), 42, 168
Nebraska
  high-risk insurance pool requirements, regulations for, 123–124
  mini-COBRA regulations in, 84
  Supplemental Security Income (SSI) and Medicaid coverage rules in, 49
  telephone numbers for health/long-term care insurance help in, 154
network model HMO, 5
Nevada
  mini-COBRA regulations in, 84–85
  Supplemental Security Income (SSI) and Medicaid coverage rules in, 49
  telephone numbers for health/long-term care insurance help in, 154
New Hampshire
  mini-COBRA regulations in, 85
  Supplemental Security Income (SSI) and Medicaid coverage rules in, 49
  telephone numbers for health/long-term care insurance help in, 155
New Jersey
  mini-COBRA regulations in, 85
  telephone numbers for health/long-term care insurance help in, 155
New Mexico
  Employee Retirement Income Security Act (ERISA) and, 60–61
  high-risk insurance pool requirements, regulations for, 125–126
  mini-COBRA regulations in, 86
  telephone numbers for health/long-term care insurance help in, 155–156
New York
  mini-COBRA regulations in, 86
  telephone numbers for health/long-term care insurance help in, 156
Nixon administration, 2

North Carolina
  mini-COBRA regulations in, 86
  telephone numbers for health/long-term care insurance help in, 156
North Dakota
  high-risk insurance pool requirements, regulations for, 127–128
  mini-COBRA regulations in, 86–87
  Supplemental Security Income (SSI) and Medicaid coverage rules in, 49
  telephone numbers for health/long-term care insurance help in, 157
Northern Marina Islands
  Supplemental Security Income (SSI) and Medicaid coverage rules in, 49
Norwood–Dingle bill, Employee Retirement Income Security Act (ERISA) and, 60
nursing care under Medicare, 24

Ohio
  mini-COBRA regulations in, 87
  Supplemental Security Income (SSI) and Medicaid coverage rules in, 49
  telephone numbers for health/long-term care insurance help in, 157
Oklahoma
  high-risk insurance pool requirements, regulations for, 128–130
  mini-COBRA regulations in, 87
  Supplemental Security Income (SSI) and Medicaid coverage rules in, 49
  telephone numbers for health/long-term care insurance help in, 157–158
open enrollment, 8, 20
Oregon
  high-risk insurance pool requirements, regulations for, 130–131
  mini-COBRA regulations in, 87
  Supplemental Security Income (SSI) and Medicaid coverage rules in, 49
  telephone numbers for health/long-term care insurance help in, 158
out of pocket amount, 8

Part A coverage (*See also* Medicare), 23–24
Part B coverage (*See also* Medicare), 24–25
Patient Protection Act, Employee Retirement Income Security Act (ERISA) and, 60

INDEX ■ 195

payment methods, 9
Pennsylvania
    telephone numbers for health/long-term care insurance help in, 158
periodic check ups, 9
Pharmaceutical Research and Manufacturers of America (PhRMA), 168
physicians
    applying for SSDI/SSI and, 57
    quality and qualifications of, 9
    selection of, 9
plan for achieving self-support (PASS), Medicaid and, 36
point of service (POS) plans, 6
pre-existing conditions, Health Insurance Portability and Accountability Act (HIPAA) and, 6-7, 64-65, 69
preferred provider organization (PPO), 3-4
    Consolidated Omnibus Budget Reconciliation Act of 1985 (COBRA) and, 74
    Medicare and, 25-27
premium, 8
prescription drugs, 16-17
    formularies (open/closed) for, 8
    free and low-cost programs, Web sites for, 165
    state pharmaceutical assistance programs for, 171
primary care case management (PCCM) program, Medicaid and, 34
primary care physician (PCP), 4, 6, 16, 17
    Medicare and, 25-26
prior authorization, 8
privacy, Health Insurance Portability and Accountability Act (HIPAA) and, 69
professional, fraternal, membership offered plans, 20

qualifying event, Consolidated Omnibus Budget Reconciliation Act of 1985 (COBRA) and, 71, 72-73

Rhode Island
    mini-COBRA regulations in, 87
    telephone numbers for health/long-term care insurance help in, 159

Section 1619b continued eligibility requirements for Medicaid, 36
See My Ad Web Site, 168
self-employed, 20
Social Security Administration (SSA), 37, 168
Social Security Disability (SSD), Medicare and, 23-24
Social Security Disability Insurance (SSDI), 36-43
    administrative law judge (ALJ) and appeals to, 40-41
    age requirements for, 37-38
    appeals on ruling for, 39-42
    applying for, 38-39, 53-58
    attorney fees for application to, 42-43
    attorneys and counsel during application process for, 41-42
    denial of claim and appeals to, 39-42
    earnings limits form, 39
    FICA tax funding of, 37
    Medicare and, 43
    Supplemental Security Income (SSI) and, 45
    trial work periods and, 43
    work credits required for, 37
sources of potential insurance coverage, 20-21
South Carolina
    high-risk insurance pool requirements, regulations for, 131-133
    mini-COBRA regulations in, 87-88
    telephone numbers for health/long-term care insurance help in, 159
South Dakota
    grievance and appeals process in, 13
    mini-COBRA regulations in, 88
    telephone numbers for health/long-term care insurance help in, 159
specialist consultations, 9
staff model HMO, 4-5
State and Local Government on the Web, 168
State Children's Health Insurance Program (SCHIP), 165, 187-188
state high-risk insurance pools, 20
    COBRA and, 93
    federal eligibility criteria for, 93
    state by state listing of requirements for, 93-142

Supplemental Security Income (SSI), 45–51
  appeals on ruling for, 48–49
  applying for, 47, 53–58
  attorney fees for application to, 51
  attorneys and counsel during application process for, 50–51
  denial of claim and appeals to, 48–49
  disability determination for, 47–48
  financial eligibility for, 45–47
  Medicaid coverage and, 31–32, 49
  residency requirements for, 45
  Social Security Disability Insurance (SSDI) and, 45
  state by state rules for coverage and, 49

Tennessee
  high-risk insurance pool requirements, regulations for, 133–134
  mini-COBRA regulations in, 88
  telephone numbers for health/long-term care insurance help in, 160
Texas
  Employee Retirement Income Security Act (ERISA) and, 60
  high-risk insurance pool requirements, regulations for, 134–135
  mini-COBRA regulations in, 88
  telephone numbers for health/long-term care insurance help in, 160
ticket to work and work incentives improvement act (TWWIIA), 91–92
  Medicaid and, 36, 91–92
  state incentives under, 91–92
tips for dealing with insurance companies, 19–20
trial work periods, Social Security Disability Insurance (SSDI) and, 43
TRICARE, 168

U.S. Marine Hospital Service, 1
Utah
  high-risk insurance pool requirements, regulations for, 135–137
  mini-COBRA regulations in, 88–89
  Supplemental Security Income (SSI) and Medicaid coverage rules in, 49

Utah (continued)
  telephone numbers for health/long-term care insurance help in, 160–161

Vermont
  mini-COBRA regulations in, 89
  telephone numbers for health/long-term care insurance help in, 161
Veterans Benefits, 168
Virginia
  grievance and appeals process in, 14
  mini-COBRA regulations in, 89
  Supplemental Security Income (SSI) and Medicaid coverage rules in, 49
  telephone numbers for health/long-term care insurance help in, 161–162

Washington
  high-risk insurance pool requirements, regulations for, 137–138
  mini-COBRA regulations in, 89
  telephone numbers for health/long-term care insurance help in, 162
Web sites of interest, 165–168
West Virginia
  mini-COBRA regulations in, 89
  telephone numbers for health/long-term care insurance help in, 162
Wisconsin
  high-risk insurance pool requirements, regulations for, 138–140
  mini-COBRA regulations in, 89–90
  telephone numbers for health/long-term care insurance help in, 163
work credits required for Social Security Disability Insurance (SSDI) and, 37
work history checklist, applying for SSDI/SSI, 57
Working Today, 20
Wyoming
  high-risk insurance pool requirements, regulations for, 140–142
  mini-COBRA regulations in, 90
  telephone numbers for health/long-term care insurance help in, 163